RALSTON CRAWFORD

Overleaf: MARINE WITH ISLAND, *oil on canvas, 32 × 40″, 1934.*

Ralston Crawford

William C. Agee

TWELVE TREES PRESS 1983

PAINTING AND VISUAL EXPERIENCE

RALSTON CRAWFORD has been identified most closely with Precisionism. His paintings of the thirties rank among the best produced by any of the Precisionists, and we are far from knowing all we should about them. Yet his Precisionist paintings occupied him for less than ten years. By 1944 his art had undergone a profound shift and expansion of style and range of feeling, and his work in painting, lithography, drawing, watercolor, etching, photography, motion pictures, and sound recording extended for more than thirty years until his death in the spring of 1978. Crawford was always a remarkably consistent painter, but, if anything, he became better after he moved beyond Precisionism. His art always has been respected, but his full development, as well as the enormous richness of his art in those thirty-odd years, has yet to be widely recognized or appreciated. Chronologically, he belonged to the same generation as the Abstract Expressionists, but because his art followed a different course, it did not receive the same attention as the painterly art of the New York School. Now that we are better able to see the entirety of art after 1945, we can begin to measure the full scope, character, and significance of Crawford's achievement.

CRAWFORD was born an American citizen in St. Catharine's, Ontario, on September 25, 1906, the son of a ship's captain who moved the family to Buffalo while Crawford was a young child. Crawford started painting, primarily as an illustrator, at the early age of fifteen or sixteen. Encouraged by a high school teacher, he decided to pursue it, since "I did such work better than anything else. . . . It seemed like the field in which I had a definite aptitude."[1] At first, he saw it as a means of earning a living, and only later did he understand and pursue the idea of "fine art."[2] By the age of fourteen, he had travelled all the Great Lakes with his father, and later he worked on ships as an able-bodied seaman. This close connection with the sea lasted his entire life and permeated his work; he later stated that "everything I see or experience in any way relates at least indirectly to my work."[3] The sea in his blood, Crawford became a restless, constant traveller both in this country and throughout the world. In 1926–1927, he sailed on tramp steamers to the Caribbean, Central America, and California, and made his first trip to New Orleans, a city which held a central place in his life and art.[4] During his trips to sea, he began to consider a life occupation as an artist.

Crawford was a largely self-educated man. His formal art training did not begin until 1927 when he landed in California, where he studied in Los Angeles at the Otis Art Institute while working as an illustrator at the Walt Disney Studios. He soon moved on to Philadelphia, the city that had spawned so many of this country's early modernist artists, where he studied from 1927 to 1930 at the Pennsylvania Academy of The Fine Arts and the Barnes Foundation. The academy's teaching was conservative for the most part, but the strong, independent voices of Hugh Breckenridge (1870–1937), whom Crawford called his "art father" who "emancipated" his ideas, and Henry McCarter (1864–1942) were important in shaping his sense of the artist's individual freedom.[5] At the Barnes Foundation, Crawford received his first extensive exposure to modern art. He was fascinated by Cézanne and Matisse, whom he termed the "giants"[6] in his background, as well as Renoir and Seurat, artists he also admired deeply. In the winter of 1927–1928, he first saw early Cubist pictures by Picasso and Braque in the collection of Earle Horter (1883–1940), the Philadelphia artist whose extensive holdings formed an important supplement to the Barnes Foundation.[7] Crawford learned to be receptive to good art, wherever he might find it, admiring quality in whatever form it might take. "Chagall, Kisling, and Laurencin were the only three modern painters who had nothing to do with any effect on my feelings," he claimed.[8] Especially important to his studies was the teaching of Dr. Barnes, which stressed the analysis of the underlying formal structure of modern art and, indeed, of all great painting. These methods in large part shaped his approach to painting, and his predilection for strong, clear structure was apparent immediately in early paintings such as *Still Life in Blue Interior* of c. 1931 (Plate 1).

During 1930–1932, he established himself in New York, the place he found most stimulating for an artist and where thereafter he always returned. He travelled in Europe in 1932–1933, looking extensively at the old masters, and came especially to admire Rembrandt and, above all, Goya, who remained a lifelong passion.[9] The sea, his earliest visual memory, yielded what he termed a "great source of visual delight"[10] in the lines and shapes of ships and their gear, rigging, sails, and ropes. It quickly established itself as a recurring theme. In *Nantucket Wharf #2*, 1932 (Plate 2), Crawford imbued the ships and buildings with the feel of Cézanne's architectonic structure, linking the shapes together by carefully organized compositional accents of the masts and rigging. These early paintings retained naturalistic details and were done in a brushed, painterly style, but by 1933 his painting increasingly was becoming simplified and broader. In the mid-thirties, he lived in rural Pennsylvania and sought for his own art motifs in rural and urban architectural views with strong inherent structures around which he could build the painting.

In 1934, Crawford did the first paintings in which his characteristic sharp-edged, planar style emerged, placing his work squarely in the Precisionist tradition begun in 1916–1917 in the art of Morton Livingston Schamberg, Charles Sheeler, and Charles

6

Demuth. In *Grain Elevators* (Plate 4) and *Ninth Avenue Elevated* (Plate 3), Crawford purged naturalistic details and brushed surfaces in favor of tightly knit, distilled planes and volumes distinguished by their clarity and openness. He was seeking, as he described it in 1939, the maximum "visual impact." He insisted that "a painting is a thing *seen*, growing out of visual experience," and was not "something to be read,"[11] aims which clearly demanded the elimination of nonessential surface incident. Although his pictorial means were refined and altered substantially this description applied to his work throughout his life. Predictably, Crawford quickly introduced images of the sea and ships into his Precisionist vocabulary, as in *Marine with Island* of 1934 (Frontispiece) and *Untitled (Ship's Prow)* of c. 1934 (Plate 5). Subject matter was fundamental to his art throughout his life. In 1941 he stated, "Certain subjects have done things to my eyes and to my head. I have painted them."[12] Because of his deep feelings for the sites he painted (he loved the city as well as the sea), he insisted that his work was "charged with emotion," that he was "never concerned with a pictorial logic to the exclusion of feeling."[13] From the beginning, then, Crawford was intent on formulating a structural art of openness and clarity which was as personal and intense as any more literally expressionist mode. He was a passionate man, and his art was filled with that passion; but he was not sentimental, and he disdained what he took to be excessive, unordered feeling.

Although Crawford's art historically has been grouped with the Precisionists, it actually owed more to European modernism than to American sources. His barn paintings of 1935 (Plate 6), which were based on direct observation, call to mind parallel concerns in Sheeler's paintings of the theme. However, Crawford's use of the motif had begun in the early thirties with paintings done in a Cézannesque manner. By 1937, in *Pennsylvania Barn* (Plate 7), Crawford had pulled the planes forward dramatically to the surface and had crisscrossed them on oblique diagonals into shallow space that created a pictorial tension quite distinct from Sheeler's development of the motif.[14]

Other pictorial currents of European Modernism were important in forging Crawford's early work: Surrealism, Cubism and Non-Objective painting. Crawford later acknowledged that Surrealism was so much in the air it was hard not to be touched by it.[15] In several paintings of the early and mid-thirties, Crawford incorporated the technique of a sharp focus on single, isolated objects, which derived from illusionist Surrealism. In *Untitled*, c. 1934 (Plate 8), for example, we feel an eerie suspension of time through the incongruous juxtaposition of a detached stairway with a cylindrical column at its top, set against a vast blue sky. Surrealist overtones also were present in the de Chirico-like stillness of Crawford's painting of 1936 *Columns with Pool* (Plate 9) which, as in all of his work, was based on a specific site, here the garden of Frank Crowninshield's residence near Wilmington. These pictorial elements, now applied to aspects of the

American landscape he had experienced, established Crawford's typical format of the thirties, a format in which the mood of de Chirico often was present. The increasing structural complexity of Crawford's barn paintings and other pictures such as *Steel Foundry, Coatesville, Pa.* (Plate 10) of 1936–1937 was furthered by his experiments in what at first appears to be almost purely abstract painting. In *Composition (Barn)* (Plate 12) of 1935, which calls to mind de Stijl and Constructivism, and in *Blue and White* (Plate 13) of 1938, a Cubist-based abstraction of intersecting planes, forms functioned as independent elements with barely discernible figurative references. The structural foundation such forms afforded later reappeared in various guises. These experiments helped shape the work of the thirties and were crucial to the evolution of his art in the early and mid-forties as it moved away from literal figuration.

Crawford, however, refrained from pursuing the full implications of his more abstract work in the thirties because he insisted that art take its roots from the world around him. Even at its most abstract, his art never was based on pure invention, but rather always could be traced to specific scenes or sites. For Crawford, abstraction was a process of selection and distillation from the known, visible world. Indeed, from 1937 until 1941, he heightened the illusionism and sculptural modelling in his painting while defining more sharply the contrast of volumes and planes. In order to emphasize the sculptural, he gravitated to sites constructed around cylindrical and volumetric masses, such as in *Coal Elevators* (Plate 14), the *Sanford Tanks* (Plate 15), both of 1938; the *Maitland Bridge* (Plate 16) series, the first two versions also dating from 1938, and *Silos* (Plate 17), of 1939. In the next two years, Crawford pushed dramatic illusionist effects to their extremes in *Overseas Highway* (Plate 18) of 1939 and *Whitestone Bridge* (Plate 19), 1940, paintings which carry us precipitously into a soaring, almost limitless space that implies a boundless future.

In 1938, following in the tradition of Sheeler and Schamberg, Crawford began photography on a serious and sustained basis, both as an integral part of his working method and as an independent art. Crawford took photographs (Estate of the Artist) of the *Sanford Tanks* and other motifs, however, not as preparatory studies in the ordinary sense, but as a kind of "nourishment" and "visual stimulation"[16] which continually allowed him to explore and discover the most powerful formal and emotive possibilities of any given site. Photography, like drawing, was a means of accumulating an ever-greater wealth of visual experience, of adding to a visual memory that seemed to retain everything. Often, photographs of a site were done *after* the painting. Or, the themes explored in a drawing or photograph were set aside, only to reappear in a painting many years later. Crawford implemented these working processes in 1942 when he began using a movie camera, a means he used more extensively in following years. (One is reminded of Léger's use of film to explore formal possibilities in his *Ballet Mécanique*). Photography

8

was a more informal, relaxed medium for him than was painting.[17] After 1934, with two exceptions, for example, he never included people in his paintings. In his photographs, however, he recorded people in all manner of station and occupation. Drawings and watercolors also contributed significantly to the evolution of his paintings. He drew endlessly, and the drawings usually were looser and more open and included far more naturalistic details than the paintings. Of them he later said:

> The drawings will, if you care to take the trip, bring you backstage. They are the record of my inquiry, my quest. They are the expression of my most private activity in picture-making, and one of the most important expressions. They are in many cases among my best work. In any case they are the immediate source of my work. . . . They are basic to my design—in a total sense.[18]

As his art matured, Crawford pushed himself to extend the boundaries of his art, to avoid what he took to be a formula or a settled look. By 1941–1942, he had become dissatisfied with illusionist modelling, in part, we may conclude, because it could capture only a single aspect of a motif's reality. In addition, he clearly had used up the possibilities inherent in the motif of brick red buildings and gray-black steel structures set against a vast blue sky that characterized his painting of the thirties. He became less interested in literal transcription and turned to a more abstract mode of painting in order to depict the many juxtapositions of experience that shaped his perception of modern life. He had come to understand that in the great traditions of the Orient and Occident, "that which is really vital, whether primitive or sophisticated," was based on "selective principles, distortion and abstraction."[19] Thus, in paintings such as *Boat and Grain Elevators* (Plate 21) of 1942, he imbued the picture with a more planar, abstract structure, although he retained distinct, if summary, figurative elements. Further, the color became far less naturalistic and began to assume a nonassociative character in its nascent stage of becoming an independent expressive force. In *Grain Elevators from the Bridge* (Plate 22), also of 1942, distant vistas were eliminated, and the structural elements were flattened radically and pulled abruptly to the picture surface. The motif still was identifiable, but Crawford constructed the picture primarily through autonomous abstract planes and patterning distilled from the subject's architectural structure. His art was on the verge of moving into the realm of Synthetic Cubist abstraction when his life and work were interrupted by the war.

HE ENLISTED in the army at the age of thirty-six in the summer of 1942. He had wanted frontline action, but eventually he was assigned to the Weather Division at the Army Air

Force Headquarters in Washington, D.C., where he became Chief of the Visual Presentation Unit. At the end of the war, he was assigned to the China-Burma and India theatre and saw many Buddhist sites, among them Ellora and Ajanta, which made an enormous impression on him. His art and life views, however, were altered profoundly by the devastation of the war and, further, by his presence at Test Able in July 1946 when the atom bomb was exploded above water in Bikini Atoll. The literal statements of unlimited optimism in technology and industry which informed his and all Precisionist painting now seemed worlds removed. They had been replaced by the recognition that destruction was one of the "dominant characteristics of our time."[20] Crisp, taut, even sleek images which referred to industry and the machine still were central to his work, but they became more ambivalent as they were forced to coexist with, and actually assimilate, themes of decay, destruction, the old and discarded, and even death, sometimes simultaneously within the same work.

In paintings such as *Bomber* (Plate 23) and *Air War* (Plate 24), for example, done in 1944 when he was able to resume some painting, Crawford incorporated powerful images of wreckage, of the aftermath of battle, that precipitated a new formal and emotive complexity in his work. In preparing visual presentations of weather patterns, he realized the pictorial potential of linear, graphic movement. These paintings incorporated multilayered elements of broken, jagged edges and twisted, disjointed lines that functioned independently of shape, area, or any descriptive role. In *Bomber*, he added a graphic, human touch—typical of Crawford—by depicting a twisted bicycle amid the massive ruins of the plane and buildings. The image of destruction in *Air War* was rendered almost completely in abstract terms, alleviated only by the presence of the dial from a smashed gauge; its abstract nature was heightened by the color which for the first time became fully nonassociative and acted as an additional formal and expressive agent.

His impressions of the test at Bikini, commissioned and then published by *Fortune* in December 1946, were depicted in *Test Able* (Plate 25) in an even more abstract language composed of smooth, curvilinear areas set against shapes with sharp edges and twisting lines, all painted in high-pitched, brilliant hues. It was an extraordinarily demanding assignment, and Crawford described his approach to recording the epic event as follows:

> These pictures constitute a comment on destruction. They most certainly do not explain the atom bomb, nor do they give quantitative information about the ships. They refer to these facts. They refer in paint symbols to the blinding light of the blast, to its color, and mostly to its devastating character as I saw it in Bikini Lagoon.[21]

One wonders whether it is beyond the powers of painting even to suggest, let alone capture, an event of such magnitude. Perhaps because of such questions Robert Coates noted the effect of the paintings was of "incongruously bright desolation—as good a commentary as any."[22] The concurrent series which depicted the wreckage of the ships' in the lagoon perhaps was more poignant, simply because it fell more readily within the scope of painting or at least within the grasp of our powers of imagination. But, characteristically, Crawford confronted the experience head on (even removing the special protection from one eye to witness the blast more directly) and then recorded it metaphorically. Once more we are given to understand Crawford's insistence that his work was charged with strongly felt emotion. This also may account in large measure for his affinity with Goya; Goya confronted the most brutal of human experience with unflinching directness, and his intensity of feeling and deeply personal response, manifested in dynamic formal relationships, was a model to which Crawford aspired.

Simultaneously with these complex images, Crawford began a series of far more condensed, open paintings which consisted of relatively few elements. Thereafter, his art alternated between these two poles; at some points, one or the other—relative simplicity and openness or relative complexity and density—clearly predominated; at other times, the two appeared simultaneously. Crawford was well aware of the polarity, for in 1946 he wrote:

> These pictures grow out of many stimuli. They vary in degree of directness of response to things seen. Some are synthetic expressions of many visual experiences, others constitute a distorted but accentuated vision of quite simple forms.[23]

This "accentuated vision" was at the heart of such superb paintings as *Sea Plane Take Off* (Plate 27) and *Weather Reconnaissance Plane* (Plate 28), both of 1946, motifs he had encountered at Bikini. The sea plane picture is a condensation of shapes abstracted from a biplane's wings and their supports, all viewed as if they were saturated by the intense, deep blues of the Pacific Ocean.

So, too, from then on Crawford's art deliberated between degrees of abstraction. We cannot recognize readily the visual source of either *Sea Plane Take Off* or *Factory with Yellow Centre Shape* (Plate 29) of 1947 without referring to the title. Yet, as noted, Crawford's painting always referred to a precise source of subject matter, although he had stated, "I don't feel obligated to reveal the forms. They may be absent to the viewer of the work, or even to myself, but what is there, however abstract, grows out of something I have seen. I make pictures."[24] Crawford insisted that the painting was an independent object "related to, but having an existence entirely apart from, the subject."[25] For example, the dynamic pictorial movement of the surface in the complex *Fisherman's Wharf, San Francisco* (Plate 30), of 1947–1950, takes on a life of its own in which we are caught up before we actually distinguish the motif, which, although containing some distilled figurative shapes, only slowly reveals itself. Or, in *Kewalo Close-Up* (Plate 31) of 1947–1948 (the result of a stay in Hawaii) the shapes appear to be autonomous, abstract elements, although in fact they are based closely on a section of a ship's bow. By contrast, in other dock scenes Crawford could shift easily back to a more clearly figurative imagery in works such as *Lobster Pots* (Plate 32) of 1958.

In his paintings of the late forties, another polarity became apparent in Crawford's art. In *Sea Plane Take Off* or *Kewalo Close-Up* the shapes were moved close to and sometimes parallel, or nearly parallel, to the surface, inducing a state of stability and calm. However, in *Minnesota Box Cars, #2* (Plate 33), 1949–1961, Crawford injected a high degree of pictorial tension by using oblique, angular shapes which often seem to collide in a contradictory spatial network that appeared to recede and advance simultaneously. Through these alternating poles we are made to feel the ambivalence of mood and point of view in Crawford's art. On one hand, the box cars no longer speak of an unquestioned faith in industrial America; rather, these myriad fractured planes suggest the rapidly accelerated, disjointed movements and tensions of a new age now at odds with itself. On the other, while we admire the pristine order of *Factory with Yellow Centre Shape*, we may experience a distinct uneasiness when reminded that the painting was based on memories of a wartime visit to the Curtiss-Wright aircraft plant in Buffalo, New York, the type of factory that delivered machines of unspeakable destruction.

With the development of these characteristics, Crawford's art of 1944–1946 was transformed into an abstracting style whose orientation can be placed within the tradition of the broad forms and strong color of Synthetic Cubism. It had evolved as a personal variant from the lineage of Picasso's art of 1917–1930, Léger's paintings of 1918–1925, Juan Gris after 1915, and others such as Jacques Villon in his work of the early twenties. In America, Crawford's post-1944 art shared certain generic relationships with the hard-edged drawing in the earlier work of artists such as Balcomb Greene, George L. K. Morris, Charles Shaw, and others associated with the American Abstract Artists group. However, his closest stylistic and thematic affinities resided with the painting of Stuart Davis (1894–1965). Davis and Crawford had met in the mid-thirties while participating in the Artists' Union and Artists' Congress, and they remained in contact. They shared a predilection for an art drawn from the "immediate experience of the tempo of life today," as Davis described it in a letter to Crawford in 1950.[26] Davis offered an important example for Crawford and numerous other American artists in the 1930s by championing the internationalism of truly modern art against the parochial claims of regionalism, and Crawford himself always stood firm in asserting the priority of international modernism. In paintings such as *Percolator* (Metropolitan Museum of Art, New York) and *Egg Beater* (Whitney Museum of American Art, New York) of 1927, Davis had demonstrated the way a personal, convincing art might be extracted from the language of Synthetic Cubism. Their work shared not only a common Cubist syntax, but also what has been described as a similar "spatial sense of the world"[27] that depicted the dynamics of modern life. Yet each artist made distinctly different types of pictures; Davis' painting, for example, generally included elements that were far more fragmented and syncopated, and his color almost always was higher-pitched. They both had the courage to pursue a style after World War II which, in the face of a wide orientation toward Surrealist-derived, painterly art, seemed to many to be almost irrelevant. Twenty years later, however, as it became apparent that Crawford's art shared common characteristics with the art of the sixties, it also became clear that his painting was part of a long, unbroken tradition of linear, hard-edged art in this country.

AFTER 1944, Crawford's art was based on a continual process of selection and synthesis, reordering and recombining of visual elements. As part of this process, Crawford introduced the method whereby places, events, colors, and shapes experienced at different times and in widely separate locales could merge in the same picture. Crawford characterized the process in 1947 by stating:

> I look to the left and to the right, ahead and behind. Then I paint from memory and from the thoughts about things I have remembered. In these recollections the last instant and many years ago are important. Perhaps it would be a difficult synthesis, but a picture referring to Pennsylvania with further reference to Nanakuli, seems possible to me.[28]

In *Elevated with Lahaina Color* (Plate 34) of 1949, for example, he combined the staccato rhythms of urban New York with the lush color of Hawaii. In successive pictures this merger of aspects of disparate places and memories was incorporated in a more general but no less potent manner. It was all part of a gradual, continuing process of visual nourishment from which he drew over the years to make his paintings.

From the late forties until the mid-fifties, the more open, relatively simpler type of painting, composed of fewer shapes, tended to predominate in Crawford's art. He again became fascinated with the structural elements of the elevated train, particularly the patterns of light and shadow they cast. In *Third Avenue Elevated* (Plate 35) of 1949, they were rendered as color shapes arranged along roughly horizontal and vertical axes, with a type of close-up abstract patterning which was far different from the distant vista he had used in his *Ninth Avenue Elevated* of 1934. Yet clearly, memories of the earlier picture stimulated the creation of a new variation of an old theme. The distilled type of picture reached its extreme in the paintings based on sails in 1955 and 1956, particularly in a 1955 painting (Plate 36) which consisted solely of two attenuated triangles in brilliant red cut into a field of deep gray-black. So, too, even in these most reductive of pictures, the motifs and their structuring depend ultimately on his earliest paintings and recollections of the sea. They also will call to mind distant yet clear overtones of similar motifs in Hartley's paintings of 1916–1917 and Demuth's of 1917–1919.

In 1951–1952, he traveled in Europe, undertook an intensive campaign of lithography (a medium he valued highly), and visited Spain, where he was captivated by the drama of the bullfight. But he was most impressed—and deeply moved—by a trip to Cologne, where he walked the bombed-out streets. Once more he recorded the horrors of World War II, now in a painting and series of lithographs entitled *Cologne Landscape*. Given the subject matter and its impact on him, the restrained quality of the few shapes in this painting may surprise us. Crawford later discussed this issue, clarifying his approach to his experiences in Cologne and Test Able:

> When man reflects what has moved him past his own personal thoughts, I feel he should reflect them as a poet and not in the same way they happened. My prints of Cologne, Germany were done because the devastating sight forced my hand to make a statement on it. Intellectually, I could not represent it in the same manner in which it had been done by others. I could not make it brutal. I wanted people to look at it as a statement they could look at again without getting ill, but never forgetting what went on there.[29]

It was perhaps this element of restraint in Crawford's painting that led James Johnson Sweeney in 1950 to characterize his art as one based on a "visual understatement" that provided the essence of the harmony in his work.[30]

Crawford frequently worked in a series, developing formal and thematic aspects of a motif in successive pictures, sometimes within a brief period, at other times over a period of years. He had begun this practice as early as 1935–1937 with the Pennsylvania barns, but it became more pronounced after 1950. In addition, he often reworked an earlier theme in the same format but in a distinctly new pictorial mode. For example, *H.M.S. Queen Mary* (Plate 37) of 1952 restated more crisply and abstractly the cropped prow of a ship that had appeared in his untitled painting of c. 1934. Although working in series had begun as a procedure in his painting, it may well have been intensified by his ever-deepening involvement with photography. From this medium he learned techniques of cropping, how to make a "prolonged study and shooting of a subject from various angles and distances," and how not to be fooled by the seemingly "final quality" of any given photograph. By these means he was sure "you will make illuminating discoveries."[31]

One of Crawford's most ambitious and extensive series—it numbered at least thirteen paintings—was devoted to New Orleans and occupied him from 1951 to 1961. Though Crawford had visited the city, he discovered its fascination in 1949–1950 while he was visiting artist at Louisiana State University. He visited frequently thereafter and took thousands of photographs of jazz musicians (like Stuart Davis he found great stimulation in jazz) and the life around them. The paintings all were based on motifs found at the St. Louis Cemetery which Edward Weston had photographed in 1941. At first they were open, flat paintings in which the forms were arranged parallel to the picture surface. *New Orleans Still Life* (Plate 36) of 1951 was based on patterns of shadows and shapes seen from a middle distance, but in *New Orleans #2* (Plate 39), *#3* (William H. Lane Foundation, Leominster, Massachusetts), and *#5* (Plate 40) of 1953–1954 he employed a close-up focus. In these paintings the dominant form was a centralized triangle which we can identify from his photographs (Estate of the Artist) as a type of metal flower holder common to this cemetery.

The field of vision expanded once more in *New Orleans #6* (Plate 41), 1955, and *New Orleans #9* (Plate 42) of 1957–1958, paintings which became more complex and irregular. In *New Orleans #11* (Hirshhorn Museum and Sculpture Garden, Smithsonian Institution, Washington, D.C.), 1957–1961, a network of linear patterning, derived from the ornamental ironwork of a gate at the cemetery, animated the entire surface and signaled an increased use of autonomous lines in subsequent work. In these paintings the colors were frequently rich blues, blacks, and grays set against a white field which clearly invoked the play of strong light and shadow against the white vault graves. (However, in another ambitious series of the fifties, the *Fishing Boats*, the color was far more personal and inventive, even idiosyncratic, and could include hues as diverse and strident as orange, green, magenta, red, brown, blue, and gray, as in *Fishing Boat #6* [Plate 44], of 1956.) Crawford by now was an enormously accomplished colorist, with his palette giving a distinctive tone to each picture through high contrast of hue and value. The New Orleans series culminated in *St. Louis Cemetery* (Plate 45), 1960, surely one of his most successful pictures. Painted in muted grays, buffs, and blues, set against a strong white and red, it was built around an almost perfect balance among flat, rectilinear areas, a curvilinear element, and irregular, almost biomorphic, shapes. The structure at the left and the coloration not only remind us of his early experiments in nearly pure abstraction, but also may suggest something of Ben Nicolson's painting. The picture's focal point is the oval wire loop from a basket of flowers, which binds the painting together while inducing an insistent movement across the surface. This pictorial variety, the contrast and harmony of structure, demonstrated Crawford's concern for what he termed "pictorial counterpoint—juxtaposing one melody or theme in relation to another."[32]

By the late 1950s, pictorial complexity predominated in his work. The *Composition* (Plates 46 and 47) series of 1958, for example, stemmed from the myriad forms he explored in the wreckage he found in a Boulder, Colorado, automobile graveyard and the *Construction* series (Plates 48, 49 and 50), also of 1958, abstracted views of a building under construction in New York. The two series were responsible for some of the most formally intricate work in his œuvre. Indeed, by both the quantity and quality of his work in 1958, it had become apparent that Crawford had reached the peak of his powers. The alternating poles of his art again were apparent when he shifted from these jarring urban rhythms to paintings which were equally complicated but which had evolved from the quiet poetry of the wharfs and the sea; both the *Lobster Pot* (Plates 32 and 51) series, begun in the late fifties, and the series of four monumental *St. Gilles* paintings (Plates 52, 53 and 54) of 1962–1963 were drawn from his memories of the French fishing village. In these paintings Crawford expanded his pictorial vocabulary to include a greater use of linear elements. These bold striations and graphic crosshatchings might indeed have stemmed, as H. H. Arnason has suggested, from the extensive work in printmaking, especially lithography, he had undertaken by that time.[33] These painterly hatch marks also may have resulted in part from many years of using it as a technique basic to his drawing. Here Crawford also reversed light and dark, negative and positive areas, as well as using solid and void interchangeably in ways perhaps suggested by his photography and his early grounding in Cubism.

Clearly, Crawford demanded from himself a continually expanding arsenal of pictorial tools in order to make pictures he did not recognize, to push himself to find through his work, as he stated it, "what my experience has been."[34] By the mid-sixties, he had achieved an extraordinary range of mood and style in his art, an art that had been nurtured by and extracted from his by then vast wealth of visual experience. Three paintings, all dating from the mid- and late sixties, vividly demonstrated just how wide that range had become and how his art could take several directions simultaneously: first, a small painting *Third Avenue Elevated #4* (Plate 55), of 1965–1968, consisted of vertical, parallel planes (Crawford worked well on a small and medium scale). It was painted in strident, almost garish colors, suggesting the neon signs which fascinated him and which he was filming extensively at this time. A second painting, *#12* (Plate 56), of 1967, referred to the sports car racing that had attracted Crawford in the early sixties. He attended major races all over the world, finding in the commitment and challenge required to handle these powerful machines an analogy to the demands and complexities of painting. Thus, in *#12* (it can be traced to drawings done in 1963), the image became a stark hierarchic emblem which virtually filled the picture and which was silhouetted against a dark field. Its streamlined newness contrasts powerfully with the desolate wreckage of the auto junk yard, one more example of the stark duality we frequently encounter in Crawford's art. In addition, Crawford intended a religious allegory, with the number twelve referring to the Apostles; notes of such allegories also appeared in other paintings at this time.[35]

As the third indication of his range, we may point to *Torn Signs* (Plate 57) of 1966–1970, also part of a series, which was composed of elongated, irregular shapes that rippled from the top to the bottom of the picture. This theme was taken from another aspect of urban life that fascinated him; it first had appeared in a photograph (Estate of the Artist) of 1939 and then in drawings of 1953–1954 before emerging in full-blown paintings in the sixties. Perhaps no other theme was digested and developed over as long a period before appearing in his painting. Unlike the Pop artists, however, Crawford took far less interest in the pristine brilliance of the typography and images of billboards. Rather, he was attracted to old, pasted-over signs on rough, weathered walls. He found that the shapes and color relationships of the signs took on a vitality with their decay, a life that he sometimes transmitted through vibrant color, as in *Torn Signs #2* (Plate 58), 1967–1968.[36]

The same range and versatility were evident within a single series. In the *Nassau* paintings, for example, also of the mid- and late-sixties, Crawford radically shifted direction with each successive picture. *Nassau #1* (Plate 59), 1966, was a study in flat architectural planes, while *Nassau #2* (Plate 60), 1968, was a magnified detail of a rope on deck uncoiling in an arabesque pattern that dominated the painting unlike any linear element had done previously. *Nassau #4* (Plate 61) of 1964–71 was a figurative, middle-distant view of a portion of a ship's prow and anchor, yet another version of a theme he had incorporated in the thirties and early fifties. It was structured more by drawing than by shaping, employing a variety of linear devices ranging from the parallel, repeated ribs of the hull to the free-form arrangement of ropes and rigging. In *Nassau #5* (Plate 62), however, Crawford takes us once more into what appears to be the realm of the more purely abstract through a series of floating, irregular forms that do not immediately suggest the world of sea and ships, although we may be sure these are the animating sources.

The type of collage effect obtained by the placement of these shapes was, nevertheless, distinct from the 1969 *Second Avenue Collage* (Plate 63), one of Crawford's most evocative paintings. Here we encounter a painting that may seem to have been literally constructed rather than painted and to consist of parts of separate pictures that have been cut and fitted together within the framing edges. Within it, we find a whole world of shifting axial and curvilinear elements that generate a distinctive pictorial animation. It appears to have been composed by the cinematic techniques of cutting and cropping that Crawford knew well from photography and his extensive film making to which he was now devoting considerable time and effort. Yet once more we discover from a photograph (Estate of the Artist) that the painting was based on a known, specific site, a wall covered with peeling theatre posters that had caught his attention. From the panorama of the wall he made blown-up detail shots that served as the basis of the painting. In its extraordinary composition, which doubtless we will find difficult to read, we are made aware of Crawford's drive to instill order within the barrage of visual stimuli that provided his impulse to make paintings. It was the order of the twentieth century, that often could create new "visual impacts and emotional continuities" based on "the sudden fade-out of the San Francisco coast and startlingly quick close-up of the beach at Honolulu. Or George Lewis and his clarinet in New Orleans and in a moment the pyramids of Mexico. And a while before these things, the cloud at Bikini."[37]

In 1969, Crawford went to Grand Coulee Dam, Washington, as one of several artists sent by the Department of the Interior to record the construction then in progress. He was so assured with the camera it was reported that he did no drawing at the site, but rather took countless photographs and shot rolls of movie film to provide sources for later stimulation.[38] In two versions of *Turbine Shafts, Coulee Dam* (Plate 64), done in 1970, Crawford depicted at close range a cylindrical mass of vertical shafts which suggested an updated version of a Precisionist theme. At the same time, however, as had become his custom, he began a series that drew on a much different type of experience. He had been attracted to Spain since his first visit in 1933; he visited again in 1952 and thereafter when-ever he could. (His attraction to Spain, to racing cars, and to the sea may remind us in some ways of Hemingway). In 1955, he visited Seville during Holy Week. It was a pro-foundly moving experience that he digested and nurtured for years, taking many photographs before he did his first painting of the theme in 1970. The theme primarily occupied him for the rest of his working life. In March 1972, he wrote that he was ab-sorbed completely by Seville, especially by the music in the cathedral and the proces-sions; he was struck particularly by the strong "relationship of sound to movement to color."[39] It is precisely these phenomena—perhaps what he meant when he said he was seeking "integration on various levels"[40]—that he apparently sought to capture in the paintings that focused on the conical hats of the *Penitentes* in the processions as the under-lying structural motif. In *Blue, Grey and Black* (Plate 65), 1973, there were a relatively few broad forms, rendered literally and composed with strong, rich color, in which we may

18

perhaps find the "hierarchy of forms" he set out to discover in any given scene.[41] In keeping with long-established patterns, the paintings became more complex and animated and concluded with works on the order of *Seville, Semana Santa* (Plate 66), 1975–1976. The painting is an abstract compilation that resonates with the waves of movement and emotion generated by the surging crowds gathered for the Holy Week, as Crawford had experienced them over many years.

"I find life handsome," he once observed.[42] Indeed, he was a man of great style whose endless quest for life informed his art at every turn. If he was a determined, independent man of enormous integrity, he was also a man of great moral and physical courage. While he was in London in the fall of 1971, doctors discovered an advanced cancer and gave him only a short time to live. Yet he did not "follow the script,"[43] as he put it, and for more than six years he worked steadily, producing some of his best and most ambitious art. He insisted on leading an active life even in his last year when he was growing weaker and could do little work; typically, he was traveling when he died in April 1978. He was buried in New Orleans in St. Louis Cemetery #3, the site that had given so much to his art, with a full brass band funeral. He would have had it no other way, and on his tombstone he had inscribed the title of a jazz tune he loved deeply, "Didn't He Ramble."

In a notebook entry of March 1977, Crawford wrote that he had come across a forgotten, untitled (and perhaps unfinished) painting (Plate 67) dated November 12, 1971. It is a small painting of irregular rust-colored forms set against a crisp blue ground, and, while it is striking, ordinarily one would by no means include it among his most accomplished or important works. Crawford saw it otherwise, and his reaction to it reveals something telling of the man and his art:

> Perhaps in no other picture of mine has there been such a rightness of relationships and color likewise, i.e., color to color and tones to colors. The shapes support the colors and tones *and* vice-versa. But none of this explains the satisfaction that I have in looking at this little picture. It is its *all-rightness* perhaps, which has an overtone I don't understand. I am glad I found that picture. In so doing, I found a bit, quite a bit, of myself.[44]

Crawford painted to discover what his experience had been, and in finding himself, through his art we may come to know something more of our own experience, of what it has meant to be an American living in the late twentieth century.

NOTES

1. Draft of letter from Crawford to a Miss Varga, June 15, 1939. Files of the Estate of Ralston Crawford, New York, hereafter referred to as Crawford Estate.

2. Interview with Mrs. Peggy Crawford, New York, March 9, 1983.

3. Undated and untitled draft of a lecture, place unknown. Crawford Estate.

4. Richard B. Freeman has championed Crawford's art for many years, and much basic information as well as valuable insights are found in his writings. See his *Ralston Crawford* (Tuscaloosa: University of Alabama Press, 1953) and *Graphics '73—Ralston Crawford* (Lexington: University of Kentucky Art Gallery, 1973). Barbara Rose, *Ralston Crawford: American Modernist* (Exhibition catalogue. St. Louis, Missouri: The Helman Gallery, May 22–June 25, 1971) offers an illuminating view of his art, particularly his relationship to the art of the sixties.

5. Statement in Ernest W. Watson, "The Art of Ralston Crawford," *American Artist*, vol. 24, no. 4 (April 1960), p. 65.

6. Transcript of interview with Edward H. Dwight; exact date unknown, but probably done in c. 1957–1958 in preparation for his exhibition at the Milwaukee Art Center in 1958, organized by Edward H. Dwight. Crawford Estate.

7. Draft of lecture at University of Minnesota, Duluth, May 1, 1961. Crawford Estate.

8. Crawford interview with Edward H. Dwight, *op. cit.*

9. Interview with Mrs. Peggy Crawford, *op. cit.* Also, in a note from a sketchbook dated October 27, 1957, Crawford wrote, "Goya looks forward to the twentieth century and perhaps beyond." Crawford Estate.

10. Crawford interview with Edward H. Dwight, *op. cit.*

11. Draft of a letter to Miss Varga, 1939, *op. cit.*

12. Statement in *A New Realism: Crawford, Demuth, Sheeler, Spencer* (Exhibition catalogue. Cincinnati, Ohio: Cincinnati Modern Art Society at the Cincinnati Art Museum, March 12–April 17, 1941), p. 5.

13. "Statements by the Artist" in Edward H. Dwight, *Ralston Crawford* (Exhibition catalogue. Milwaukee, Wisconsin: Milwaukee Art Center, February 6–March 9, 1958), p. 12.

14. He was close friends with Niles Spencer and Louis Guglielmi and while he deeply admired their work he was not directly influenced by it. See Crawford's tribute to Spencer in Richard B. Freeman, *Niles Spencer* (Lexington, Kentucky: University of Kentucky Art Gallery, 1965), pp. 19–20.

15. Statement as quoted by Russell Lynes, *Ralston Crawford* (Exhibition catalogue. Washington, D.C.: Middendorf/Lane Gallery, December, 1977). It also should be noted that something of a parallel is found in de Chirico's influence on Léger in 1924. Also, writing in the catalogue of Crawford's exhibition held at the Santa Barbara Museum of Art in 1946, Donald Bear noted the "super-real" quality in Crawford's work as well as a "certain magic in the abrupt shock" of his use of space, pointing out that Crawford appeared to be well aware of the later work of Mondrian and the earlier paintings of de Chirico.

16. The two terms run throughout Crawford's writings and statements, and he called his films of the sixties "Nourishment of the Artist."

17. Interview with Mrs. Peggy Crawford, *op. cit.* See Norman Geske, *The Photography of Ralston Crawford* (Exhibition catalogue. Lincoln, Nebraska: Sheldon Memorial Art Gallery, University of

Nebraska, 1974), and Edith A. Tonelli and John Gossage, *Ralston Crawford: Photographs/Art and Process* (Exhibition catalogue. College Park, Maryland: The Art Gallery, University of Maryland, 1983).

18. Letter to Richard B. Freeman, October 1972, quoted in Freeman, *Graphics '73—Ralston Crawford, op. cit.*, p. 11.

19. "Ralston Crawford Comments on Art," *Paradise of the Pacific,* vol. 59, no. 8 (August 1947), p. 18.

20. Statement in "Paintings of Operation Crossroads at Bikini" (Exhibition brochure. New York: The Downtown Gallery, December 3–21, 1946).

21. *Ibid.*

22. Robert M. Coates, "The Art Galleries: The Artist and the World," *The New Yorker,* vol. 22, no. 44 (December 14, 1946), p. 105.

23. Statement in Exhibition catalogue, Santa Barbara Museum of Art, 1946, *op. cit.*

24. Statement in Russell Lynes, *op. cit.*

25. Statement as quoted by H. H. Arnason, *Ralston Crawford* (Exhibition catalogue. New York: Lee Nordness Gallery, March 12–30, 1963), no pagination. This catalogue especially is useful for its study of the paintings.

26. Letter from Stuart Davis to Ralston Crawford, February 17, 1950. Crawford Estate.

27. Interview with Mrs. Peggy Crawford, *op. cit.*

28. "Ralston Crawford Comments on His Art," *Paradise of the Pacific, op. cit.*

29. Statement in *Ralston Crawford—1971* (Exhibition catalogue. Cincinnati, Ohio: Contemporary Arts Center, 1971), p. 4.

30. James Johnson Sweeney, "Introduction," *Ralston Crawford* (Exhibition catalogue. Baton Rouge, Louisiana: Louisiana State University, February 24–March 17, 1950).

31. "Ralston Crawford Explains His Photography," *Modern Photography*, vol. 13 (September 1949), pp. 74–78, 110. In this article Crawford also explained how various scenes and sites were fused in a single painting from photographs and drawings.

32. "Statement by the Artist," in Edward H. Dwight, *Ralston Crawford*, 1958, *op. cit.*, p. 11.

33. Arnason, *Ralston Crawford*, 1963, *op. cit.*

34. Ralston Crawford voice-over statement in film, *Ralston Crawford, Painter,* produced by Neelon Crawford, 1973.

35. Reported by Mrs. Crawford, *op. cit.*, and by John Crawford, the artist's son, in a note to the author, April 7, 1983. The cross often appeared in the guise of a telephone pole or power line in earlier works and certain of the *New Orleans* series.

36. "Torn Posters," undated manuscript. Crawford Estate.

37. Statement quoted in Richard B. Freeman, *The Lithographs of Ralston Crawford* (Lexington, Kentucky: University of Kentucky Press, 1962), pp. 22–23.

38. See John DeWitt, "Reclamation Launches Art Program," *Reclamation Era,* vol. 56, no. 1 (February 1970), p. 7. In April 1973, he made his fourth trip, writing to Virginia Zabriskie, his dealer at the time, that he had "seen enough to paint thirty pictures." Zabriskie Gallery files, New York.

39. Letter to Virginia Zabriskie, March 29, 1972. Zabriskie Gallery files, New York.

40. "Statements by the Artist," in Edward H. Dwight, *Ralston Crawford, op. cit.*, p. 9.

41. Statement in film, *Ralston Crawford, Painter, op. cit.*

42. Undated draft of a talk, place unknown. Crawford Estate, *op. cit.*

43. Letter to Virginia Zabriskie, May 10, 1975. Zabriskie Gallery files, New York.

44. Notebook, March 1977. Crawford Estate, Inventory #60.9.

PLATES

All photographs, unless otherwise noted, are from the Estate of Ralston Crawford, courtesy of Robert Miller Gallery, New York.

"I was lucky enough to come in contact with fine modern painting during my student days. Cézanne, Renoir, Matisse, Braque, Picasso, Gris. I did not reject it. It constituted my basic nourishment."

Statement from a lecture for the Student Awards Dinner at the University of Illinois, Lincoln, May 23, 1966. (All manuscripts quoted from are in the files of the Estate of the Artist).

"When I was a student at the Barnes Foundation, with its really superb collection, I was most attentive to the work of Cézanne and Matisse. Matisse is an artist that I have thought of less frequently in recent years, but his expression was of tremendous importance to me. Perhaps these two artists, more than any others, influenced my development. Matisse's ideas about colour stimulated my own searches. Cézanne deeply affected my entire attitude toward painting. I speak of the early influences, because the early ones really count. The total list would almost be endless. At this time I mention a few words: Prado, Duncan Phillips, Rijksmuseum, Ellora, Ajanta."

Statement from *Ralston Crawford* by Edward H. Dwight (Exhibition catalogue. Milwaukee Art Center, February 6–March 9, 1958), pp. 11–12.

1. STILL LIFE IN BLUE INTERIOR, *oil on canvas, 10¼ × 8¼", c.1929.*

"Like many young painters, I wandered, speculated. Sometimes I didn't have a dollar, no, not even a quarter. Still, would I be as good as Cézanne? As Matisse? But in a moment I realized the vain character of this speculation. I went on looking for myself. I realized that a kind of historical paralysis could set in, fatally, if we did otherwise. Still I was far from naive enough to believe that my art would ever be *all* mine. I wasn't living in an old house boat in a dried-up river bed. I was in the midst of a lot of action. I learned wherever I could and my indebtedness to many artists of many times is great indeed.

I had my masters and I wasn't afraid to look up to them. I haven't seen the statement in 35 years but I think I remember the gist of it. 'Don't worry about your originality, if you haven't got it, there's not much you can do to get it; if you've got it, there's not much you can do to lose it.' Robert Henri said something like that."

Statement from a lecture for the Student Awards Dinner at the University of Illinois, Lincoln, May 23, 1966.

2. NANTUCKET WHARF #2, *oil on board, 12 × 14"*, 1932.

"While I was born in Canada, I have lived most of my life in this country. So in a general way I am an American—British flavour. But I have never been concerned in any way with putting an American or un-American stamp on my work. . . .

. . . Reference to influences is made without regret or apology. I consider indebtedness to other artists highly desirable.

If art *is* important, how could the man who produces it (and surely he considers it important), willingly turn away from the production of other artists of the past and present?"

Statement from a draft of a lecture at the University of Minnesota, Duluth, May 1, 1961.

3. NINTH AVENUE ELEVATED, *oil on canvas, 20 × 16", 1934. Private Collection.*

4. Untitled [Grain Elevators], *oil on canvas board, 9 × 12″, c.1934.*

"To go back to the sea, I remember lines in one of O'Neill's plays, *Long Day's Journey Into Night*, where he talked about the 'Dawn Watch'; I never heard it called that before but I know the watch that he is referring to. He refers to the four to eight watch in the morning which is also in effect in the evening. He talked about the beauty he found standing that watch. It was there I suppose that a particular kind of solitude related to color and movement were perhaps my deepest and most meaningful early experiences in relation to painting. . . . There was the color, and the intensely human character of many of the situations, involving my ship. Sometimes for a very young man, scarcely more than a boy, the action was a little bit frightening. It was rather rough existence in many ways. Yet, it was this as I say, intensely humanizing. As one crossed the sea, and looked at the ship's gear, the rigging, everything about it was, for me, a source of visual delight. This was intensely nourishing in terms of specific visual experience. Then there was the courageous speculative character of the men living this life. . . . They were very high rollers and high rolling is essential to picture-making."

Statement from a transcript of an interview with Edward H. Dwight; exact date unknown, but probably done in c. 1957–1958 in preparation for his exhibition at the Milwaukee Art Center in 1958, organized by Edward H. Dwight.

5. UNTITLED [SHIP'S PROW], *oil on canvas, 40 × 32″, 1934.*

"Cézanne was a mountain in my young life and still is."

Statement in *A New Realism: Crawford, Demuth, Sheeler, Spencer* (Exhibition catalogue. Cincinnati, Ohio: Cincinnati Modern Art Society at the Cincinnati Art Museum, March 12–April 17, 1941), p. 5.

"I have no creed or manifesto. They are traps. Yet some of the more interesting sound tracks for painting have been done by painters. Therefore I say a few things about my attitude toward painting. These comments may heighten the communicative function of that painting.

I speak first of subject-matter, because for me it is of basic importance. Certain subjects have done things to my eyes and to my head. I have painted them.

The form? I make an unfashionable statement: I feel closer to Cézanne, Seurat, Modigliani, Gris, and Picasso than to Ryder, Eakins and Homer.

I do not pour my painting into any mold, but use the formal knowledge I have gained to express what I feel and think. I have never been interested in playing little paint games for my own amusement. I get excited about painting and when I feel that I have said something it is important that it be said to someone. No vacuums. Yes, the function, the communication is the thing."

Statement in *A New Realism: Crawford, Demuth, Sheeler, Spencer* (Exhibition Catalogue. Cincinnati, Ohio: Cincinnati Modern Art Society at the Cincinnati Art Museum, March 12–April 17, 1941), p. 5.

"I arrived at my own form, on the basis of a long and patient search, though I did not look for style. Style for me is part of the super structure. One arrives at it, or he doesn't. It is a matter of his clarity of conviction. To this day I am unconcerned with painting pictures that are recognizably mine. To be sure my search has a specific direction and my paintings indicate that direction."

Statement from a lecture for the Student Awards Dinner at the University of Illinois, Lincoln, May 23, 1966.

6. PENNSYLVANIA BARN, *oil on canvas, 25 × 30", 1935.*

7. PENNSYLVANIA BARN, *oil on canvas, 30 × 36", 1937. Courtesy Blum-Helman Gallery, New York.*

"It was in this city, New York, 1930–1934, that I commenced to find myself, because, contrary to the current enthusiasm for regionalism, it was, and still is, the most stimulating place for many painters, and I think that any painter should have fairly large doses of New York—while not necessarily doing the bulk of his work here."

Statement from a draft of a letter to Miss Varga, dated June 15, 1939.

8. UNTITLED [COLUMN ON STAIRS], *oil on canvas, 16 × 24″, 1934.*

9. Columns with Pool, *oil on canvas, 30 × 36″, 1936.*

10. STEEL FOUNDRY, COATSVILLE, PENNSYLVANIA, *oil on canvas, 32 × 40″, 1936–1937.*
Collection of Whitney Museum of American Art, New York.

11. ROOF, 31 WEST 11TH STREET, *oil on canvas, 34 × 40″, 1934.* Collection Edward R. Downe, Jr., New York.

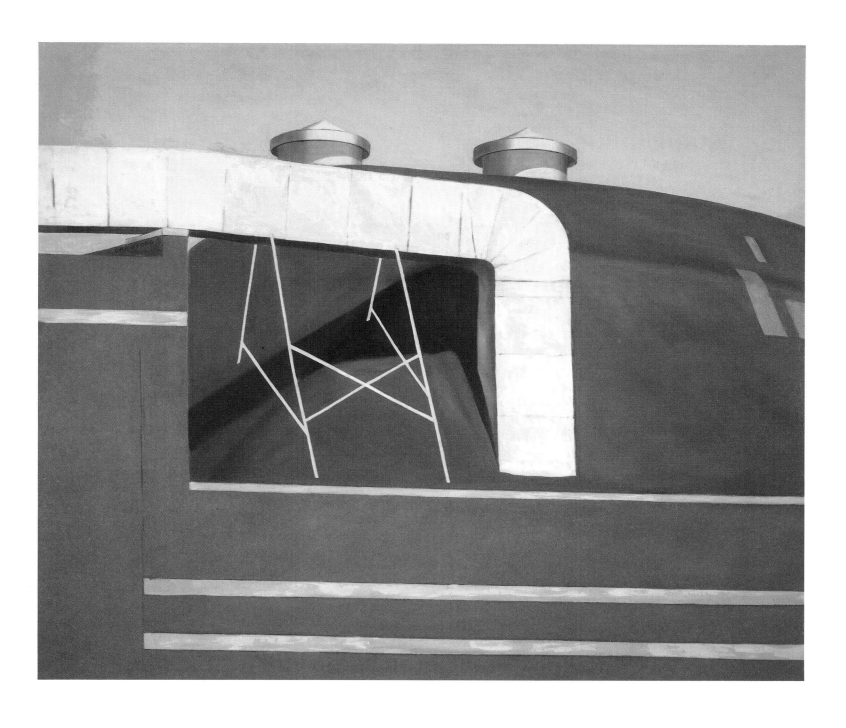

12. COMPOSITION (BARN), *oil on board, 10 × 8″, 1935.*

13. BLUE AND WHITE, *oil on board, 8 × 10″, 1935.*

"Yes, I would say that in general I was optimistic. I was interested then in painting and drawing in the same way that Goya was interested in it. *Everything* mattered in terms of his personal responses, but once the act was started I don't think it mattered to him whether he was doing a picture of a massacre or of a nice little child with a bird on a string. This was the way I felt about painting. I wouldn't say 'let the "content" be damned,' or 'let the "audience" be damned,' but content and audience were secondary considerations. And so, all together, I still think that your word 'optimism' applies. The problem of the '30s for us young painters seemed indeed clearer than today's. We thought the solutions were around the corner. Optimism, for some of us, was the note. . . .

. . .Yes, I'm 98 percent certain that *Coal Elevators* was done when I was living in Exton, Pennsylvania, which was at that time hardly more than a crossroads between Paoli and Downingtown. I was living there, but I used to go into Philadelphia, and I remember, with rather notable clarity, that I stopped to make some drawings of these coal elevators . . . at least drawings that pertained to the coal elevators. But the more I look at the painting now, the more I realize (and I haven't seen it in a good while) the great extent to which it deviates from the things seen . . . .

. . . For example, I have painted many pictures which utilize something I can call a 'blank center.' I would say that *Coal Elevators* is probably close to one of the best in this category. . . .

. . . You ask about the drawing, and I answer *yes*, an emphatic *yes*. . . . Drawing has always been tremendously important to me in many, many ways and I feel very sorry for artists today who don't draw. It's often such a pleasure. I draw nearly every day now . . . it's at least as important to me as practicing the scales on a piano is to the pianist. It means that and something more. Drawing is an exploration in which I may find nothing. Sometimes it's an exploration in which I find something which is sufficiently satisfying, and I have no subsequent interest in painting. Often I'll make ten or fifteen drawings with reference to a painting, yet not make the painting. That's when something doesn't come off. Perhaps I don't crystallize enough, or I crystallize too much. And you can be too clear about these things. There is more than one kind of tracing and if one is too clear, even in his own head, the picture he makes will be tracing a completed mental image and that's a bad kind of picture, as far as I'm concerned.

A principle that I still hold is that the transition of color within an area is less important than the relationship of that area to another. Now this has always been my position and I found that my concerns and interests could be best kept under control with what is in some ways a relatively lean style, in terms of manipulation of pigment. My paintings have been called 'without nuance' . . . but in *Coal Elevators* the relationship of one form or tone to another indicates my great interest in nuance."

Statements from an interview with Jack Cowart in "The Collections; Recent Acquisition: *Coal Elevators*, by Ralston Crawford." St. Louis Art Museum *Bulletin* (January–March 1978), pp. 10–15.

14. COAL ELEVATORS, *oil on canvas, 36 × 50", 1938.*
The St. Louis Art Museum, gift of Mr. and Mrs. Richard T. Fischer.

"Sometimes I photograph a single subject with a whole roll of film in a Leica, Contax or Rolleiflex—the choice being determined by what I am trying to do. These many shots may mean no more in relation to the final photograph than a few pencil lines would mean in relation to a completed oil painting. But, by making numerous exposures, you learn not to be fooled by the seemingly final quality of any photo that appeals to you. You learn to ask yourself if it might not be better to take it from another angle in another way entirely; later on, you are inspired to print the same negative in a variety of sizes and croppings. This is not drudgery, but an interesting activity all the way. You will make illuminating discoveries."

Statement from Ralston Crawford, "Ralston Crawford: A Modern Artist Explains the Relationship Between his Photography and Painting," *Modern Photography*, vol. 13, no. 1 (September 1949), pp. 74–79.

15. SANFORD TANKS, *oil on canvas, 36 × 28", 1938. Joseph Helman, New York.*

"More than ever it is necessary for the painter to consider precisely the possibilities and limitations of his medium. For if he does not, he may wake up and find himself doing things that can be done better by the radio, motion-picture, still-photograph, etc. Yes, everyone is supposed to know about the camera, but I still see a lot of paintings that look like Kodachromes—out of focus, and perhaps not too well exposed. Also the renaissance of the middle-west has left me somewhat unimpressed. The professional virility, and affected naivete of much of this work seems definitely something to be outgrown.

The criterion seems to be that if the picture shows no European influence, it is then, ipso facto—splendid. Obviously this is fallacious. No painter of to-day, American or otherwise can ignore the vast contributions of the European artists of the last fifty years—or 350 years. This knowledge is to be assimilated by the American painter just as the American psychologist, physicist, or engineer uses the contributions of his European contemporaries.

To be more specific concerning my own work, I believe that the importance of the visual impact of the picture, or the experience that makes the picture, must be further emphasized. A painting is a thing *seen*, growing out of a visual experience. It is not some thing to be *read*, and a painter has no business presenting compositional fumbles, any more than a writer writing a language he does not understand, or a writer trying to write paintings. I want to remember content, but also to remember that I am speaking the language of a painter."

Statement from a draft of a letter to Miss Varga, dated June 15, 1939.

16. MAITLAND BRIDGE, *oil on canvas, 32 × 40", 1938. Private collection.*

17. SILOS, *oil on canvas, 16 × 20″, 1939. Stolen from The Helman Gallery, St. Louis, Missouri, 1975. Photograph courtesy Blum-Helman Gallery, New York.*

RC: "I remember at this particular point on the causeway I felt I was quite literally going to sea in my car. And amazingly enough, many years later when I was on my way to India I had a similar feeling—of crossing the desert on a ship when we went through the Suez Canal.

It wasn't just the twist of the visual imagery which amused me. The title was from the immediate sensation.

I suppose one of the reasons for the severity of some of my paintings is that I am in many respects an incurable romantic. But I could never conceive of reducing my painting to a slobber. I am long on feeling, and a lot of discipline—or steering of that feeling—is necessary. When I painted *Overseas Highway* as a young man I did see an awful lot of space before me and it fascinated me. The perspective is used simply as a vehicle in relation to that space."

JC: "It's either romantic or surreal. The other aspect of these timeless, unexpected vistas or sections is that they are opposed to your present work and the work in between."

RC: "Indeed, it has a surreal quality. That's incontestable. There are many pictures I've made which indicate my interest in Surrealism at that time. It was not my primary concern, but it was also not an inconsequential concern."

Statement from an interview with Jack Cowart in "The Collections; Recent Acquisition: *Coal Elevators,* by Ralston Crawford." St. Louis Art Museum *Bulletin* (January–March 1978), pp. 10–15.

"This painting constituted a rather special experience in my painting and the response to it has been rather special, . . . that is the painting called the *Overseas Highway.* I can remember my work on that painting, it was almost like writing. I put it right down, I didn't change anything basically in the design in the painting. I drew it, as I frequently do, I always do a certain amount of drawing on the canvas before I start to paint, usually always with charcoal. I had worked in this manner, put down my drawing and I proceeded to paint on it. That was it. There were no problems in relation to it. The continuing painting was simply as a matter of giving me paint quality, more substance."

Statement from an untitled transcript of an interview with Joan Simon, exact date unknown but probably c. 1971. The Greenberg Gallery, St. Louis, Missouri, reel 3, p. 4.

18. OVERSEA'S HIGHWAY, *oil on canvas, 28 × 45", 1939.*
Private collection. Photograph courtesy Hirshl & Adler Galleries, New York.

"Ralston Crawford constructs an exhilarant vision of this world of modern technology wherein space and speed are disciplined, controlled and structurally measured by the mind of man. He achieves a new note of clarity through his use of lucid color and near-abstract design. He bridges that seemingly impossible distance between the pictorialist and the non-objective or abstract artist. He warms his empty vistas by an almost perfectly adjusted color sense. He abstracts his design of the shapes and patterns of things only to reconstruct them with a swift, succinct and super-real quality. Too, there is a certain magic in the abrupt shock of his use of space. It would appear that Crawford is more than well aware of the underlying human imagination that motivated the later compositions of Piet Mondrian and the earlier paintings of de Chirico."

From Donald Bear, *Ralston Crawford* (Exhibition catalogue. M.H. de Young Memorial Museum, San Francisco, May 4–June 4, 1946), pp. 2–3.

19. WHITESTONE BRIDGE, *oil on canvas, 40 × 32″, 1940.*
Memorial Art Gallery of the University of Rochester, New York ; Marion Stratton Gould Fund.

20. At the Dock, *#2, oil on canvas, 30 × 36″, 1942.*

"These pictures grow out of many stimuli. They vary in degree of directness of response to things seen. Some are synthetic expressions of many visual experiences, others constitute a distorted but, accentuated vision, of quite simple forms. . . . It is perhaps well to think of the pictures in terms of future experience made possible through contact with a vital contemporary pictorial vision."

Artist's statement in Donald Bear, *Ralston Crawford* (Exhibition catalogue. M.H. de Young Memorial Museum, San Francisco, May 4–June 4, 1946), pp. 2–3.

21. BOAT AND GRAIN ELEVATORS, *oil on canvas, 30 × 36", 1942.*

"I belong to the twentieth century. To me, it is very important to belong to the century in which one lives. I have observed and considered at great length contemporary activities with a further consideration of appropriate pictorial procedure. It is clear to me that the forms of the Italian Renaissance as well as the Victorian viewpoint, for example, are not adequate for modern visual comment."

Statement from Ralston Crawford, "Comment on Modern Art by the Artist." *Paradise of the Pacific*, vol. 59, no. 8 (August 1947), pp. 17–19, 32.

22. GRAIN ELEVATORS FROM THE BRIDGE, *oil on canvas, 50 × 40", 1942.*
Collection of the Whitney Museum of American Art, New York; gift of the Friends of the Whitney Museum of American Art, 1963.

"My work is usually charged with emotion, and not of a basically geometric character. I realize this comment is quite at variance with many responses to my pictures, but I am never concerned with a pictorial logic to the exclusion of feeling. For me, the shape relationships are right only when they feel right, as well as look right. Still, an approach to painting which has analytical properties is very important to me. I believe that good paintings are done by and for people who do resort to the use of reason, along with having a concern with their feelings. The genesis of my pictures varies greatly. They are complete when they express a synthesis of my emotions and ideas. What happens between their genesis and completion is a long story."

Statement from Edward H. Dwight, *Ralston Crawford* (Exhibition catalogue. Milwaukee Art Center, February 6–March 9, 1958), pp. 9–10.

23. BOMBER, *oil on canvas, 28 × 40", 1944.*

24. AIR WAR, *oil on canvas, 16 × 22″, 1944.*

"Destruction is one of the dominant characteristics of our time. These pictures constitute a comment on destruction. They most certainly do not explain the atomic bomb, nor do they give quantitative information about the ships. They refer to these facts. They refer in paint symbols to the blinding light of the blast, to its color, and mostly to its devastating character as I saw it in Bikini Lagoon.

However, it is futile to look for illustrative value in each detailed area. My purpose has been to convey ideas and feelings in a formal sequence, and not to reproduce nature."

Statement from *Ralston Crawford ; Paintings of Operation Crossroads at Bikini* (Exhibition catalogue. The Downtown Gallery, New York, December 3–12, 1946), pp. 2–3.

"RC: . . . But now I had to go out and see, at Bikini, the essence of it. Perhaps I should say the 'new' essence.

JC: Did you feel that this was sheer physical destruction, or was it moral destruction?
RC: Moral and physical.
JC: The implications of the whole act.
RC: Yes, the implications were there indeed—and the likelihood of a coming moral breakdown."

Statement from an interview with Jack Cowart in "The Collections; Recent Acquisition: *Coal Elevators*, by Ralston Crawford." St. Louis Art Museum *Bulletin* (January–March 1978), pp. 10–15.

25. TEST ABLE, *oil on canvas, 24 × 18", 1946.*
Georgia Museum of Art, The University of Georgia ; Eva Underhill Holbrook Collection, gift of Alfred H. Holbrook, 1946.

26. BIKINI, TOUR OF INSPECTION, *oil on canvas, 24 × 34″, 1946.*

"If you refer to the great traditions in the art of the Orient and the Occident, you will find that which is really vital, whether primitive or sophisticated, is not concerned with copying nature. It is based on selective principles, distortion, abstraction. Such principles have functioned for the purpose of conveying feelings and ideas of considerably greater significance than a specious appeal to your vanity and sentimentality."

Statement from Ralston Crawford, "Comment on Modern Art by the Artist." *Paradise of the Pacific*, vol. 59, no. 8 (August 1947), pp. 17–19, 32.

27. SEA PLANE TAKEOFF, *oil on canvas, 16 × 12¼", 1946.*

28. WEATHER RECONNAISSANCE PLANE, *oil on canvas, 10¼ × 14″, 1946.*

"The times I have started without a direct physical reference point are very few. And it doesn't matter to me if the source is clear to the person looking at the picture, if there is some kind of residue, a fertilizing residue, of this initial experience. If it hasn't got that, it's sterile, at least in my opinion. I've never had any inclination to reduce painting to a series of repeated angles or curves. In relation to my work, I'm not congenial to the use of the term 'geometric.'"

Statement from an interview with Jack Cowart in "The Collections; Recent Acquisition: *Coal Elevators*, by Ralston Crawford." St. Louis Art Museum *Bulletin* (January–March 1978), pp. 10–15.

29. FACTORY WITH YELLOW CENTRE SHAPE, *oil on canvas, 28 × 40", 1947.*

"I am interested in form that grows out of feeling, a form that articulates, steers that feeling. This steering involves the intellect."

Statement from an untitled, undated manuscript by Crawford.

30. FISHERMAN'S WHARF, SAN FRANCISCO, *oil on canvas, 30 × 40″, 1947–1950.*
Private collection.

"I am not interested in literary description, yet in all my things I make reference to subject matter, though it frequently does not show itself. I always start from something. As James Johnson Sweeney said, 'nothing begets nothing.'"

As quoted by Russell Lynes in *Ralston Crawford* (Exhibition catalogue. Middendorf/Lane Gallery, Washington, D.C., December 1977). Reprinted Century Association, February 28–April 2, 1978, p. 1.

31. KEWALO CLOSEUP, *oil on canvas, 22 × 34¼″, 1947–1948.*

32. Lobster Pots, *oil on canvas, 24 × 18″, 1958.*

"I started this painting in Baton Rouge, Louisiana, and I worked on it perhaps, three hours a day for probably three weeks, and I marvelled at the fact that each day's work seemed to make the painting worse. . . . I really went backwards at a terrific speed in that picture, and I remember that the only reason that I brought it back to New York was that it was an expensive piece of canvas on a rather well-made stretcher, very good stretcher. If it hadn't been for that, I would have chucked it in a fire, if I would have been able to find a fireplace large enough for this size painting. That's the trouble with painting these super king size ones, they are very difficult to burn. . . . I brought it back up here and I can't say that it annoyed me or that it was a specter in my studio but I'd get it out once in a while and I'd think about it and I put it away again. . . . I started to work on it again, I suppose because I am a poor loser. I just don't like to lose and so I worked on the painting. I think, and as far as I know, it is one of the most successful pictures I've done. Everything is under control and I've had that grimly amusing experience a couple of times of having people mention that it appears to have been done with such ease which is not common for people to say about any of my pictures, but they seem to find that in this one. I don't tell them the story, because they might get awfully tired."

Statement from an untitled transcript of interview with Joan Simon, exact date unknown but probably c. 1971. The Greenberg Gallery, St. Louis, Missouri, reel 3, p. 3.

33. MINNESOTA BOXCARS #2, *oil on canvas, 60 × 40", 1949–1961.*

"I look to the left and to the right, ahead and behind. Then I paint from my memory and from the thoughts about the things I have remembered. In these recollections the last instant and many years ago are important. Perhaps it would be a difficult synthesis to establish, but a picture referring to Pennsylvania, with further reference to Nanakuli, seems possible to me."

Statement from Ralston Crawford, "Comment on Modern Art by the Artist." *Paradise of the Pacific*, vol. 59, no. 8 (August 1947), pp. 17–19, 32.

34. ELEVATED WITH LAHAINA COLOR, *oil on canvas, 22 × 32", 1949. Harvey Rambach, New York.*

"My photography follows my painting in a great measure. So it is in general of a rather abstract variety. To be sure, there is some interaction. A few years ago, the idea of working from photographs was considered 'inartistic.' Now many painters recognize photographs as an informative, stimulating source to be incorporated with other experience. The pictures on pp. 76–77 illustrate in a measure the value that they have for me. They are in no way a subtitute for one's experience in viewing various objects. Rather they are an extension of that experience. They magnify and clarify other observations. They are sometimes used in relation to my drawings and color studies as sources of specific information concerning the movement of light patterns in relation to the possible effect on picture structure. On many occasions I use the camera as a sketch pad. The endless variations on a theme such as the 'El' picture on page 75 were suggested with a 36 exposure roll of 35mm film. Also the various formal combinations arrived at through the enlarging (with various croppings) of a single negative are highly informative."

Statement from Ralston Crawford, "Ralston Crawford: A Modern Artist Explains the Relationship Between his Photography and Painting." *Modern Photography*, vol. 13, no. 1 (September 1949), pp. 74–78, 110.

35. THIRD AVENUE EL, *oil on canvas, 29 3/4 × 40 1/8", 1949.*
Collection of Walker Art Center, Minneapolis, gift of the T. B. Walker Foundation.

"When I got beyond my school days, playing the scales with paint brushes, and started to think about what really counted with me, I remembered the waterfronts, my own many voyages at sea, as very important experience. At sea the quality of feeling in direct contact with forces bigger than oneself is frequently present. It has always seemed to me that such indirect experiences, remote in some ways from actual picture-making, are the basic nourishment for the artist. He learns how to paint. Every year the art schools turn out many accomplished technicians. But they must be nourished and fed by broader experience. For me, this business of going to sea was a tremendous part of it."

Statement from Edward H. Dwight, *Ralston Crawford* (Exhibition catalogue. Milwaukee Art Center, February 6–March 9, 1958), pp. 11–12.

36. THE SAILS, *oil on canvas, 14 × 11", 1955.*

"Selection is the base of all art. Nothing comes of nothing. Everything in an artist's work is drawn from the world outside him save the energy to discover, prefer and combine. None but poor paintings—or poor poems, for that matter—are trustworthy as factual records of an artist's experience. The essence of artistic beauty is harmony within the work, not truth to the life which begat it. And what guides an artist in his selection remains the essential signature of his work—something which will make its appearance consistently in every realized work of an authentic artist.

This is strikingly evident in Ralston Crawford's art. Not only in his paintings, drawings and lithographs, but in his photographs as well. And this is the proof of the prime importance of selective vision. For in Crawford's work we recognize the same vocabulary of shapes in the camera's mechanically and chemically achieved records, as in the products of the painter's free hand. Behind both lies the eye. And behind the eye the energy to discover, prefer and combine shapes suggested by the outer world towards the compassing of a consistently sought-after inner harmony.

But what characterizes this harmony which gives Crawford's work the individuality we recognize throughout—even in such widely different media as the photograph and oil painting?

Perhaps the term 'visual understatement,' if one may be permitted to use it, would provide the most suggestive description. Nothing overstressed. The eye never sated. The onlooker is always left with an appetite for just a slightly warmer tone, for a stronger, a slightly more emphatic line. Still each of these minor understatements is

37. H.M.S. QUEEN MARY, *oil on canvas, 24 × 16″, 1952.*

related to other understatements throughout the canvas: an avoidance of compositional crowding that balances on the verge of emptiness—an emphasis on perspective
lines that never bores a hole into the picture's surface and flat areas of colour that lie
parallel to the face of the canvas, but always seem to float, never quite settle down,
dead, against it. In all Crawford's best work we have this provision of subtle, delicate
tensions. From the homely materials from which he derives the suggestions for his
pictures, we are led to expect a banal and lifeless effect; and we are always surprised by
the atmosphere of unfamiliarity he gives the eventual outcome through this understatement, this elimination of certain details—this selection.

And the result, this signature we spoke of which marks all his fully realized paintings, graphic work and photographs—the basic aim of his selective approach is a cool,
unworldly, or, perhaps more exactly, other-worldly calm. Not a haunted, paralyzed,
dream calm such as we find in the empty perspectives of Giorgio de Chirico, not the
sultry calm of saturated color areas in Léger's strong, simple compositions, nor the
warm intensity of Mondrian's; but a quiet, reticent, lyric ease. In fact, the final picture
is often more reminiscent of the movement and shapes of water plants in a pool than
of the harsh, forbidding contours of industrial forms out of which Crawford's picture
have ostensibly sprung.

Selection is the first step. But only the beginning. The artist must be a creator, the
maker of a new object. And on this primary base, his gift for selection, so evident in all
Crawford's work, we see him realize that further stage: a self-contained entity—a
painting."

James Johnson Sweeney, *Ralston Crawford*. (Exhibition catalogue. Louisiana State University Art Gallery,
Baton Rouge, February 24–March 17, 1950)

38. NEW ORLEANS STILL LIFE, *oil on canvas, 30 × 45", 1951.*

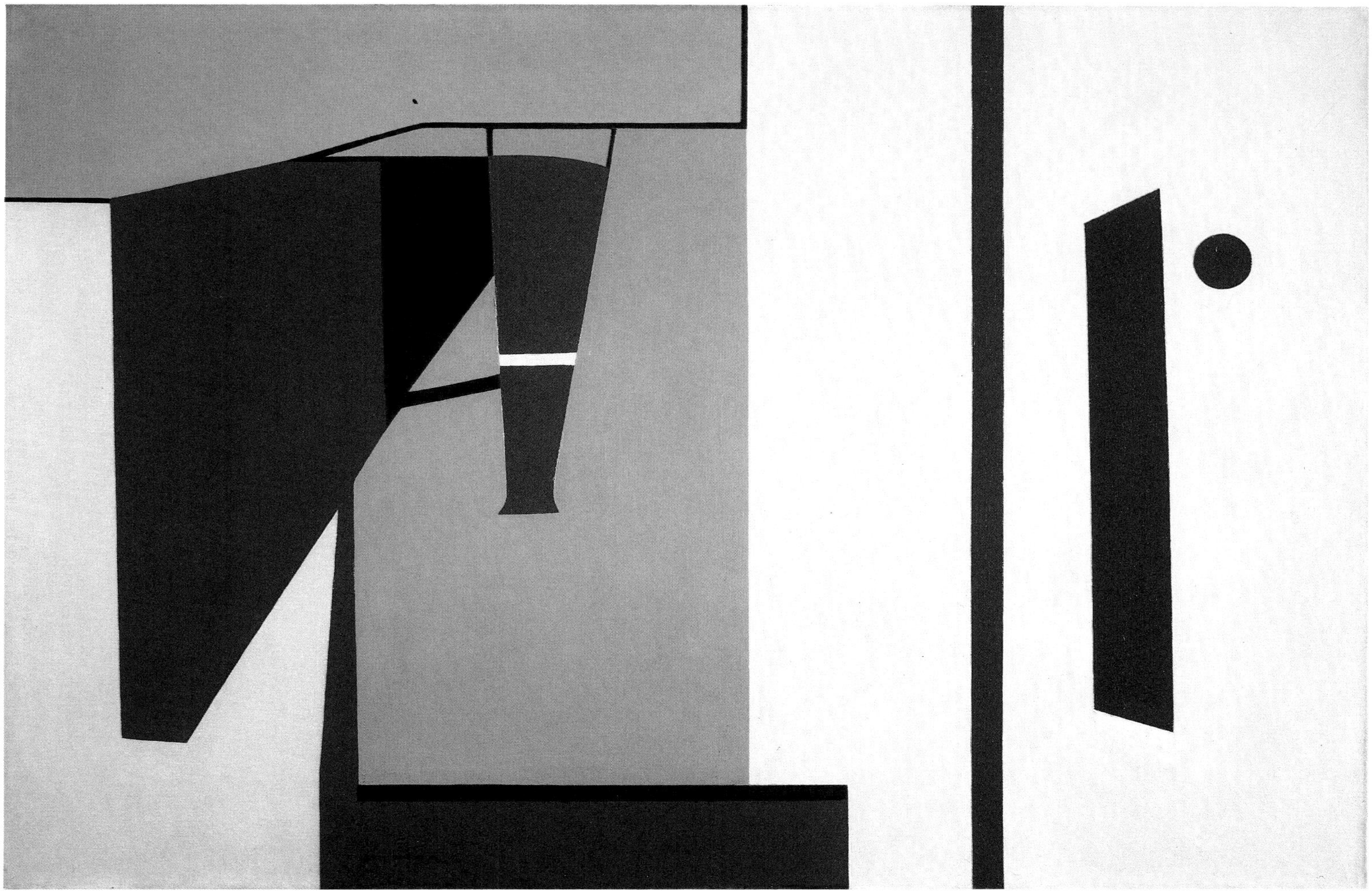

"Whenever I have been abroad, the thought that there is a New Orleans in America has always eased the idea of returning. This city is not simply 'interesting' or 'stimulating,' but an object of my affection. The music is a part of the New Orleans I love. I must emphasize that my interest in the music is related to a particular social context. . . .

. . . Being a painter I am often asked if I find any specific relationship between jazz music and my painting. I would say that the two expressions have one thing in common—they place a great deal of emphasis on the importance of individual expression, and the spirit and forms of New Orleans music, being good things, feed my work because they nourish me. But this is a general stimulation, like the work of the matador, Carlos Arruza, or the Buddhist cave temples of India, each of these things expressing interests quite different from that of modern European or American painting."

Statement from Ralston Crawford, "Ralston Crawford's Photographs," *The Second Line*, vol. 4, no. 7–8 (July–August 1953), cover and pp. 1–12. Includes photographs of jazz musician.

39. NEW ORLEANS #2, *oil on canvas, 40 × 30", 1953. Mr. Maurice Vanderwoude. Photograph by John A. Ferrari.*

"My pictures mean exactly what they say, and what they say is said in colours and shapes. This doesn't mean that immediate communication with anyone is at all inevitable. When I have taken a big step forward, the picture seldom looks right to me. Sometimes it takes me several days, or even weeks, to accept the validity of my own discovery. Maybe this thought is important to people looking at pictures. I am sure they have a problem when a picture says something new. It is easier to accept the familiar expression, but it can be rather boring—at least eventually."

Statement from Edward H. Dwight, *Ralston Crawford* (Exhibition catalogue. Milwaukee Art Center, February 6–March 9, 1958), pp. 11–12.

40. NEW ORLEANS #5, *oil on canvas, 50 × 36¼", 1953–1954.*
Sheldon Memorial Art Gallery, University of Nebraska, Lincoln; J. M. Hall Collection, 1956.

"I've never concerned myself very much with the universal's relation to painting. In moments which I presume must be described as religious ones, I may well have been concerned with such things—but in general, not in my painting."

Statement from an interview with Jack Cowart in "The Collections; Recent Acquisition: *Coal Elevators*, by Ralston Crawford." St. Louis Art Museum *Bulletin* (January–March 1978), pp. 10–15.

41. New Orleans #6, *oil on canvas, 13 × 18¼", 1955. Private collection, Washington, D.C.*

"My basic concern in looking at pictures, and in making them, is with integration on various levels. Certainly Pascin, for example, would have made a mistake, if he had attempted to paint on Goya's plane, and yet I would not deny the fact that he did find an integration, not profound, but a gesture, an expression in paint that was worth putting down. So it is often irrelevant to say that a picture does not have a particular kind of depth. Further, it is futile to look for superficial entertainment in a work of great substance.

I think this range—pictures integrated on various levels—also exists in the output of one artist. At least, it should. Even great men can't be great every day. Yet it's pretty difficult for a man to divorce himself entirely from the dictates of his time. Certainly pressures exist in this country today that are not conducive to the presentation of a variety of expression from one artist (or even a notable variety within large groups). So we find a great deal of uniformity. This is no virtue, but indicates the use of a formula. Today the trademark is, for many, a mighty important thing, and it affects the attitude of many museum directors, many painters and art dealers who frequently want paintings that can be recognized as the work of a particular artist at a distance of 200 feet. This is not stimulating. It is a lid on their work. I am more pleased when I have made a picture that does not look like my previous work, that is not recognizable."

Statement from Edward H. Dwight, *Ralston Crawford* (Exhibition catalogue. Milwaukee Art Center, February 6–March 9, 1958), pp. 9–10.

"Presently, I find stimulation in the bullfight, and jazz music. The matador's range of expression, alone in a ring with a murderous bull, is a very great thing to watch. As one of the English writers on the subject has said, it is not to be classified as a cruel sport, but rather a cruel method of creating great plastic beauty. It is also an activity in which the spectator is present for the actual creation of the work of art. Another art that is new each time is jazz music, as it is now played in New Orleans, as a part of a broad, profound, social expression. These expressions are, for me, deeply humanizing."

Statement from Edward H. Dwight, *Ralston Crawford* (Exhibition catalogue. Milwaukee Art Center, February 6–March 9, 1958), pp. 11–12.

42. NEW ORLEANS #9, *oil on canvas, 19¾ × 28¾", 1957–1958.*

43. FISHING BOAT #3, *oil on canvas, 18 × 15", 1955.*

"To say that the marine forms of the Great Lakes, the blue of the Caribbean, the light of California, Florida, Mexico, India, various islands of the Pacific, the West Indies, the bull fights in Spain, the Grand Prix car racing in various parts of Europe, motorcycle racing at Daytona, the music of New Orleans, the wines of Burgundy, the caves at Ajanta, Ellora . . . 12th- and 13th-century Catalonian art in Barcelona, Goya, Rembrandt, Matisse, Cézanne, Picasso, the people I have loved, the people who have given me support in my work, are all in this picture, is true."

Statement from an untitled, undated manuscript by Crawford.

44. FISHING BOATS *#6, oil on canvas, 40 × 20", 1956.*

"I am very much interested in a kind of pictorial counterpoint—the juxtaposing of one melody or theme in relation to another, or to several. It is out of this argument or contrast that I believe interest is created in pictorial structure. This must be part of the total plan—I am uninterested in producing the decorative."

Statement from Edward H. Dwight, *Ralston Crawford* (Exhibition catalogue. Milwaukee Art Center, February 6–March 9, 1958), pp. 11–12.

45. St. Louis Cemetery, New Orleans, *oil on canvas, 30 × 22", 1960. William Janss, Sun Valley, Idaho.*

"Back to Colorado: sometime ago I found in Boulder the largest assembly of wrecked automobiles that I have ever seen. I went to this junk pile many times. In truth, the shapes I found there were indeed more interesting than the new cars. The unpredictable relationships of broken, torn and twisted automobile parts, plus the startlingly unique quality of the individual shapes called for all of my attentiveness. In my continuing line of consciousness they were of course related to the plane wrecks of World War Two and to my recollection of Bikini, where I saw Test Able.

The positive nature of seeing transcended the dreary connotations of these shapes. In short my reaction was one of extreme pleasure. I am quite certain that this picture will in no way affect the automobile accident rate. Such motivation is out of my field. But I will be pleased if it provides for the person seeing it some of the satisfaction that I got from viewing the wrecked cars."

Statement from an untitled, undated manuscript.

46. COMPOSITION #3, *oil on canvas, 26 × 36″, 1958.*

47. COMPOSITION #4, *oil on canvas, 12 × 18″, 1958.*

48. CONSTRUCTION #2, *oil on canvas, 24 × 36, 1958. Peggy Crawford.*

"In all good paintings there is the possibility of real experience that goes far beyond any simple pleasure principle. I believe that my own attitude toward everything and everyone is different, richer, because I have been in the caves of Ellora and Ajanta and because I have seen the great Catalonian frescoes in Barcelona. Since my paintings offer no qualitative information regarding the visual situation to which they are related, can they be classified simply as designs? If by designs you mean something we find on window curtains or playing card backs, no. If you mean design, a planned organization of my thoughts and feelings, then, yes, they are designs, abstract designs, abstracted from my experience—linked to measurable concrete reality."

Statement from a draft of a lecture at University of Minnesota, Duluth, May 1, 1961.

49. CONSTRUCTION #5, *oil on canvas, 24 × 36″, 1958.*

50. CONSTRUCTION #8, *oil on canvas, 24 × 36″, 1958.*

"I believe I quote William James more or less correctly, at least in general substance:
—forms remain forever, they may lose their individual character but they are inde-
structible—like the shapes on a much used blotter!"

Statement from an untitled, undated manuscript.

51. LOBSTER POTS #3, *oil on canvas, 45 × 60", 1962–1963.*

"I have had an opportunity not only to see the many changes in these forms, but to look at myself looking at the forms. Then, too, one may think of New Orleans at Croix-de-Vie, and this makes for another kind of painting. Since these pictures, like most of my other pictures, do little to document the scenes, they would probably be disturbing, or unsatisfactory, to the fisherman or the space salesman in the cemeteries. My interest is in assembling in my paintings a satisfying variety of colour shapes that will constitute a unified whole.

My interest in art in general has to do with its civilizing effect through stimulating our sense of fitness—the rightness of certain relationships. These relationships are basically important in all human existence. As Bosanquet put it in a rather droll manner; the ears of a beautiful spaniel transferred to the head of a beautiful woman would not make an aesthetically pleasing view."

Statement from a draft of a lecture at University of Minnesota, Duluth, May 1, 1961, p. 12.

52. St. Giles #1, *oil on canvas, 30 × 40", 1962–1963.*

"On the subject of search: This is the heart of the matter. The organization of my own faculties: my intuition, my intelligence, my love and my faith for the purpose of creating a form satisfying to me because of its relationship to the faculties I have mentioned and related to that which I find positive and beautiful in my life."

Statement from a lecture for the Student Awards Dinner at the University of Illinois, Lincoln, May 23, 1966.

53. ST. GILES #3, *oil on canvas, 24 × 36", 1962–1963.*

"TIME: When I am able to annihilate it, I am in the right groove. For me any consciousness of time is akin to anxiety. When I am *really* working, I have a hundred years—forever—to complete the painting. When there is no time sense, the pictures are inclined to grow quickly."

THE PLAN, the approach: For me excessive reflection can have a paralysing effect. The relationship of the act of painting to the thought, the preceding thought, is a matter of very delicate balance. Sometimes one goes over the picture, mentally, before it is started, until it is stale, and then still-born.

THE STIMULATION: My whole life. When I am in my best form, everything I see or experience in any way relates, at least indirectly, to my work. I think it was the composer Varese who said that some artists need a stomach pump, others a gusher cap. I usually need the latter. Every picture I make calls for a dozen more."

Statement from a lecture for the Student Awards Dinner at the University of Illinois, Lincoln, May 23, 1966.

54. ST. GILES #4, *oil on canvas, 45 × 60", 1965–1968.*

55. THIRD AVENUE ELEVATED #4, *oil on canvas, 10 × 8″, 1965–1968.*

"[I would] rather have present a grand prix car race and possibly a drawing by Ingres. . . . the sensitivity, knowledge and general organization of the racing driver may raise questions as to who is really intelligent."

Statement from an untitled, undated manuscript.

56. *#12, oil on canvas, 16 × 20″, 1967.*

"I have long, under certain circumstances, enjoyed the bill boards, posters, electric and neon signs and of course the pasted over weathered walls of Paris and sometimes New York. This is indeed popular art not to be confused with 'pop art.' The latter is not popular art at all, but an academic. . . .

To go back to the posters, as I was saying, I like them most when they are torn, pasted over. The bromidic shape and colour relationships take on a vitality with their decay. At any rate I see relationships that are highly stimulating and informative in connection with my own paintings.

Sometimes the rubbish or junk car lots are similarly interesting to me."

Statement from "Torn Posters," undated manuscript.

57. TORN SIGNS, *oil on canvas, 60 × 40", 1966–1970.*

58. TORN SIGNS #2, *oil on canvas, 60 × 45″, 1967–1968.*
Hirshhorn Museum and Sculpture Garden, Smithsonian Institution, Washington, D.C.

59. NASSAU #1, *oil on canvas, 20 × 30″, 1966. Courtesy Richard York Gallery, New York.*

60. NASSAU #2, *oil on canvas, 18 × 30", 1968.*

61. Nassau #4, *oil on canvas, 30 × 45″, 1964–1971.*

"The public, the museums, and the critics have been generous toward my work. And when I believe that I have shared my pictures with *anyone*, I am happy. But the pictures are not painted for any audience. They represent my particular journey."

Statement from a lecture for the Student Awards Dinner at the University of Illinois, Lincoln, May 23, 1966.

62. NASSAU #5, *oil on canvas, 30 × 40", c.1965.*

" 'I don't feel obligated to reveal the forms. They may be totally absent to the viewer of the work, or even to myself, but what is there, however abstract, grows out of something I have seen. I make pictures.' "

As quoted by Russell Lynes in *Ralston Crawford* (Exhibition catalogue. Middendorf/Lane Gallery, Washington, D.C., December 1977). Reprinted, Century Association, February 28–April 2, 1978, p. 1.

63. SECOND AVENUE COLLAGE, *oil on canvas, 40 × 30", 1969.*

64. TURBINE SHAFTS, COULEE DAM, *oil on canvas, 22 × 16″, 1970.*

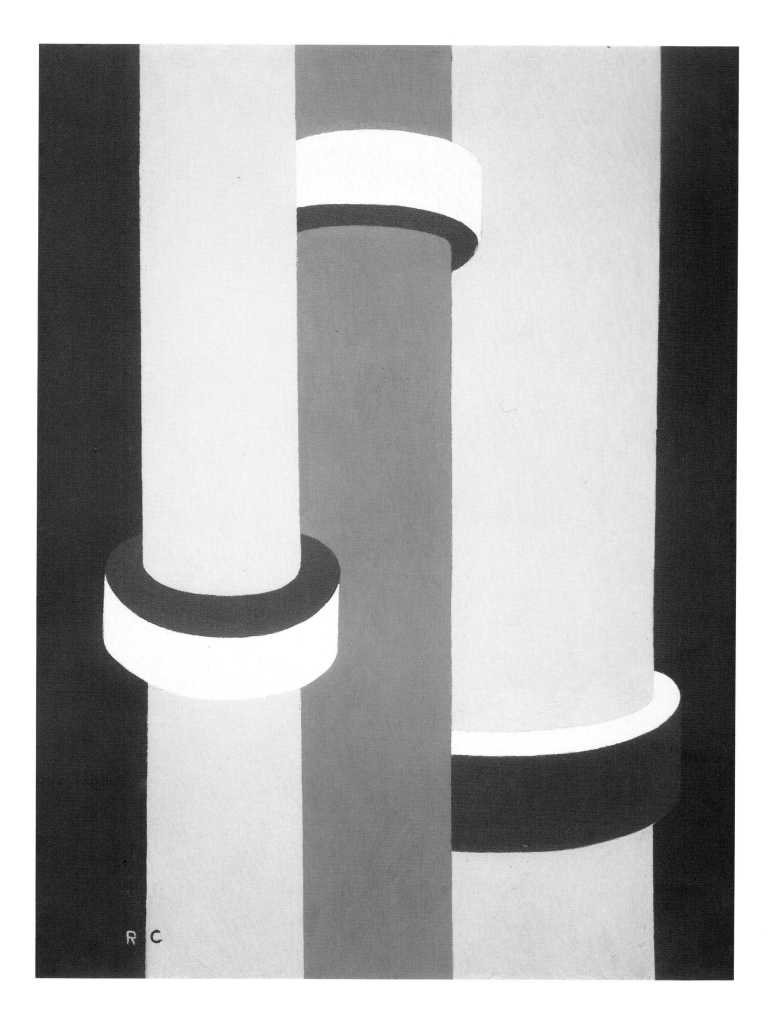

"There is within me a passionate need to perform to the utmost of my ability. Anything less seems against the moral law.

I have little interest, really none, in making the kind of pictures I know how to make. In such a procedure there is for me no enlightenment."

Statement from an untitled manuscript, May 7, 1964.

65. BLUE, GREY, BLACK, *oil on canvas, 50 × 36", 1973.*

"The 'subject matter' is never limited to a single visual impact or idea. Indeed it is a picture of the other pictures one has seen, of one's response to his time, one's recollection of his friends, their stimulating and enlightening remarks, or it is the smile, the handshake, the voice that may nourish us for years and will contribute to the form of the picture. This diffusion grows more complex as we continue to live. How are we to sort out such subject matter? I neither know nor care."

Statement in a letter to Richard B. Freeman, dated December 30, 1963 and reprinted in Richard B. Freeman, *Graphics '73 Ralston Crawford* (University of Kentucky Art Gallery, Lexington, February 11–March 4, 1973), p. 8.

66. SEVILLE, SEMANA SANTA, *oil on canvas, 38 × 50", 1975–1976.*

67. UNTITLED, *oil on canvas, 16 × 24", 1971. Peggy Crawford.*

CHRONOLOGY, BIBLIOGRAPHY, EXHIBITIONS AND COLLECTIONS

Compiled by Terence F. Eagleton.

RALSTON CRAWFORD: CHRONOLOGY

1906   Born September 25 at St. Catharine's, Ontario, Canada. Father, a ship's captain, was a naturalized American citizen.

1910–1926   Lives in Buffalo, New York. Travels Great Lakes with father during vacations from school; works in a factory, at a soda fountain, as an architectural draftsman, and in road construction.

1926–1927   Sailor on tramp steamers to Caribbean, Central America, and California. First trip to New Orleans. Studies at Otis Art Institute, Los Angeles. Works in Walt Disney's studio, illustrating *Oswald the Rabbit*.

1927–1930   Studies at the Pennsylvania Academy of The Fine Arts in Philadelphia and Barnes Foundation, Merion, Pennsylvania. Awarded two scholarships at the Pennsylvania Academy.

1930–1932   Paints in New York. Awarded a Louis Comfort Tiffany Foundation Fellowship, Oyster Bay, New York. Summers, studies at the Hugh Breckenridge School, East Gloucester, Massachusetts. Marries Margaret Stone. October 28, 1931, Edward Alden Jewell, in *New York Times* review of group show at Hotel Marguery, singles out Crawford for his "solidly constructed landscapes."

1932–1933   Travels in Europe. Studies at Academies Colarossi and Scandinave, Paris. Travels in Spain, Italy, and Balearic Islands.

1933   Studies at Columbia University, New York.

1934   First one-man show, Maryland Institute of Art, Baltimore.

1935   Edward Alden Jewell, *New York Times*, April 1, in review of Society of Independent Artists exhibition, singles out Crawford, noting that he is striving honestly for a style of his own. Also singled out in same show by Henry McBride, *New York Sun*, April 13.

1934–1939   Paints in Chadds Ford and Exton, Pennsylvania.

1936   Henry McBride, "The Annual Independent Show," *New York Sun*, May 2, singles out Crawford and Stuart Davis as the "two best abstract painters in the show."

1937–1938   Awarded Bok Fellowship to the Research Studio, Maitland, Florida. First sustained experience with photography. Travels to New Orleans.

1940   In New York, produces paintings, book illustrations, and book jackets.

1940–1941   Visiting instructor at the Cincinnati Art Academy, first of many teaching jobs during his career; loves the travel and stimulation in teaching. Important exhibition, *A New Realism: Crawford, Demuth, Sheeler, Spencer,* Cincinnati Modern Art Society, Cincinnati Art Museum.

1942   Visiting instructor, Albright Art School, Buffalo, New York. Purchase Prize for color lithographs at The Metropolitan Museum of Art, New York. Marries Peggy Frank, formerly director of the Cincinnati Modern Art Society. Enlists in the 603rd Engineers Camouflage Battalion, United States Army.

1943–1945   Master sergeant, chief of the Visual Presentation Unit of the Weather Division, Headquarters, Army Air Force, Washington, D.C.

1945   Assigned to China, Burma, India theaters. Trips to Ajanta, Ellora, Borivli, Elephanta, Bud-Gaya, Puri, and other sites in India.

1946   Awarded Army Commendation Ribbon. Sent by *Fortune* as eyewitness to atomic bomb Test Able, Bikini Atoll.

1947   Guest director, Honolulu School of Art, summer session.

1948–1949   Instructor, Brooklyn Museum Art School. Visiting instructor, Art Academy of Cincinnati and University of Minnesota, Minneapolis.

1949–1950   Visiting artist, Louisiana State University, Baton Rouge.

1950   Photographs in Mexico. Goes on lecture tour to 28 colleges in the United States. Takes first of many trips to New Orleans, photographing and documenting the lives of black jazz musicians.

1951–1952   Travels in Europe. Intensive work in lithography in Paris. Visits Cologne, Germany. Visiting artist, University of Colorado, Boulder.

1952–1957   Faculty member, New School for Social Research, New York.

1953   *Ralston Crawford* published by Richard B. Freeman, University of Alabama Press, Tuscaloosa. Important retrospective exhibition, University of Alabama. Visiting artist, University of Michigan, Ann Arbor.

1954–1955　Lives in Paris and Croix de Vie, France. Intensive work in lithography and painting. Trip to Spain to observe Goya's paintings and bullfights.

1955　One-man exhibition of lithographs at Weyhe Gallery, New York, and Los Angeles County Museum of Art.

1956　Goes on lecture tour for American Association of Colleges.

1957　In France, works in lithography and painting. Takes another trip to Spain.

1958　Important retrospective at Milwaukee Art Center. Visiting artist, University of Colorado, Boulder. Discovery of large automobile graveyard leads to series of paintings entitled *Compositions*. One of ten artists commissioned by Wolfson Construction Company to do interpretation of building being erected at 100 Church Street, New York; leads to series of paintings entitled *Constructions*.

1959　Travels to Spain and Paris for additional lithography.

1960–1962　Faculty member, Hofstra College, Hempstead, New York.

1960　Visiting artist, University of Kentucky, Lexington, and University of Southern California, Los Angeles.

1961　Appointed photographic research consultant, Archive of New Orleans Jazz, Tulane University, New Orleans. Visiting artist, University of Minnesota. Major exhibition, *The Precisionist View in American Art,* organized by the Walker Art Center, Minneapolis.

1962　Travels to Greece, Egypt, and France, producing lithography and photography. *The Lithographs of Ralston Crawford* published by Richard B. Freeman, University of Kentucky Press, Lexington.

1962–1968　Attends Grand Prix car races frequently in Europe and United States.

1963　Travels to Scandinavia, Germany, North Africa, Ireland, and Scotland.

1964　Travels to Trinidad and Tobago, Maine, and Norway.

1965　Visiting artist, Sheldon Memorial Art Gallery, University of Nebraska, Lincoln.

1966　Visiting artist, University of Illinois, Champaign. Travels to Ireland, Isle of Mann, England, France, Germany, and Denmark.

1967　Travels to England, Spain, and Denmark.

1968   Travels to Guadeloupe, Martinique, Orkney and Shetland Islands. Important retrospective exhibition at Creighton University Fine Arts Gallery, Omaha, Nebraska.

1969   Paints in New York. Travels, paints, and produces motion picture photography in Madrid, Pamplona, and Seville, Spain; Tangier and Fez, Morocco. Shows *Various Depths* at the Creighton University Film Festival, Omaha, Nebraska. Travels to Grand Coulee Dam, Washington, on behalf of Bureau of Reclamation, U.S. Department of the Interior.

1970   Works in New York. Travels to Seville for Holy Week. Receives cash award from National Academy of Arts and Letters.

1971   Travels to Seville, Pamplona, London, and the Outer Hebrides. In London, doctors discover he has cancer. Shows three short films, *Torn Signs, Room 333, Big Bayou Black,* at The St. Louis Art Museum.

1972   Travels to Seville for Holy Week, later to North Africa, Madrid, London, Isles of Harris and Lewis in the Outer Hebrides, Lisbon, Madeira, Seville. Receives Edwin Palmer Memorial Prize, National Academy of Design.

1973   Travels to Grand Coulee Dam and South Pacific (Fiji Islands, Pago Pago, Tonga Islands, Suva, and Hawaii). Travels to Europe, Norway, Scotland, England.

1974   Travels around the world: Canada, Tahiti, New Hebrides, New Guinea, Bali, Indonesia, Singapore, Bangkok, New Delhi, Nepal, Afghanistan, Frankfurt, Paris, London.

1976   Travels to England and Italy. Executes first series of etchings in Italy.

1977   Travels to New Orleans.

1978   Dies April 27, Houston. Buried in St. Louis Cemetery, New Orleans.

RALSTON CRAWFORD: SELECTED BIBLIOGRAPHY

A New Realism: *Crawford, Demuth, Sheeler, Spencer.* Organized by the Cincinnati Modern Art Society (later the Contemporary Arts Center) at the Cincinnati Art Museum, March 12–April 17, 1941.

Adams, Philip Rhys. *Crawford, Cutler.* Cincinnati Art Museum, February 16–March 15, 1949.

"Air Transport." *Fortune*, vol. 31, no. 4 (April 1945). Cover by Crawford.

Arnason, H. H. *Ralston Crawford.* The Nordness Gallery, New York, March 12–30, 1963.

Bear, Donald. *Ralston Crawford.* The Santa Barbara Museum of Art, April 2–May 2, 1946. Exhibition traveled to M. H. de Young Memorial Museum of Art, San Francisco, May 4–31, 1946; Portland Art Museum, Oregon, August 18–September 15, 1946; and the Seattle Art Museum, Washington.

"Bikini: Documentary Photographs, Abstract Paintings, and Meteorological Charts." *Fortune*, vol. 34, no. 6 (December 1946), pp. 151–161. Illustrations by Crawford.

Cowart, Jack. "Recent Acquisitions: *Coal Elevators,* by Ralston Crawford." The St. Louis Art Museum *Bulletin*, vol. 14, no. 1 (January–March 1978), pp. 10–15. Interview with Crawford.

Crawford, Ralston. "A Modern Artist Explains the Relationship Between His Photography and Painting." *Modern Photography*, vol. 13, no. 1 (September 1949), pp. 74–78, 110.

Crawford, Ralson. "Ralston Crawford's Photographs." *The Second Line*, vol. 4, nos. 7–8 (July–August 1963), pp. 1–12.

De Witt, John. "Reclamation Launches Art Program." *Reclamation Era*, vol. 56, no. 1 (February 1970), pp. 5–8.

Dwight, Edward H. *Ralston Crawford.* Milwaukee Art Center, February 6–March 9, 1958. Includes "Statements by the Artist."

Erskine, The Hon. Robert M. *Ralston Crawford.* St. George's Gallery Prints, London, 1958. Foreword to catalogue.

Ford, Ford Maddox. *Ralston Crawford's Pictures.* Boyer Galleries, Philadelphia, March 10–30, 1937. Introduction to catalogue.

Freeman, Richard B. "Artist at Bikini." *Magazine of Art*, vol. 70, no. 4 (April 1947), pp. 156–158.

Freeman, Richard B. *Graphics '73 Ralston Crawford.* University of Kentucky Art Gallery, Lexington, February 11–March 4, 1973. Exhibition traveled to National Collection of Fine Arts, Smithsonian Institution, Washington, D.C.

Freeman, Richard B. *Ralston Crawford.* Tuscaloosa: University of Alabama Press, 1953.

Freeman, Richard B. *The Lithographs of Ralston Crawford*. Lexington: University of Kentucky Press, 1962.

Freeman, Richard B. *The Work of Ralston Crawford*. Flint Institute of Arts, Michigan, June 1942.

Geske, Norman. *The Photography of Ralston Crawford*. Sheldon Memorial Art Gallery, University of Nebraska, Lincoln, January 15–February 10, 1974. Exhibition traveled to Montgomery Museum of Fine Arts, Alabama, February 19–March 17; Munson-Williams-Proctor Institute, Utica, New York, March 31–April 28.

Jerde, Curtis D., and Lawrence, John H. *Music in the Street: Photographs of New Orleans, by Ralston Crawford*. The Historic New Orleans Collection, New Orleans, April 13–July 22, 1983.

Koch, Vivienne. "Four War Drawings." *New Directions #9*. New Directions Books, Norfolk, Connecticut, 1946.

Lubbers, L. E. *Ralston Crawford: Retrospective Exhibition*. Creighton University Fine Arts Gallery, Omaha, Nebraska, October 23–December 9, 1963.

Lynes, Russell. *Ralston Crawford*. Middendorf/Lane Gallery, Washington, D.C., December 1977.

"New Orleans Report." *Le Jazz Hot*, no. 62 (January 1952), pp. 21–24. Photo essay by Crawford.

"Photographs by Ralston Crawford." *Directions*, vol. 3, no. 3 (March 1940).

"Radar—The Technique." *Fortune*, vol. 32, no. 4 (October 1945). Cover and illustrations pp. 138–145 by Crawford.

Ralston Crawford—1971. Contemporary Arts Center, Cincinnati Art Museum, 1971.

"Ralston Crawford Comments on Art." *Paradise of the Pacific*, vol. 59, no. 8 (August 1947), pp. 17–19, 32.

Rose, Barbara. *Ralston Crawford: American Modernist*. The Helman Gallery, St. Louis, May 22–June 25, 1971.

Simon, Jean. "New York Today: Some Artists Comment." *Art in America*, vol. 65, no. 5 (September–October 1977), pp. 80–81. Includes interview with Crawford.

Sweeney, James Johnson. *Ralston Crawford*. Louisiana State University Art Gallery, Baton Rouge, February 24–March 17, 1950.

"Thunder over the North Atlantic." *Fortune*, vol. 30, no. 5 (November 1944). Illustrations pp. 153–160 by Crawford.

"The Merchant Marine." *Fortune*, vol. 30, no. 5 (November 1944). Cover illustration by Crawford.

Tillim, Sidney. "In the Galleries: Ralston Crawford." *Arts Magazine*, vol. 36, no. 1 (October 1961), pp. 39–40.

Tonelli, Edith A., and Gossage, John. *Ralston Crawford: Photographs/Art and Process*. The Art

Gallery, University of Maryland, College Park, March 22–May 1, 1983. Exhibition traveled to The Frederick S. Wright Art Gallery of University of California at Los Angeles, September 27–November 13.

Von Groschwitz, Gustave. *Lithographs—Ralston Crawford*. Contemporary Arts Center, Cincinnati Art Museum, January 1956. Foreword to the catalogue.

Watson, Ernest W. "The Art of Ralston Crawford." *American Artist*, vol. 24, no. 4 (April 1960), pp. 47–51, 64–66.

Wolf, Ben. "Crawford Interprets Bikini Blast." *The Art Digest*, vol. 21, no. 5 (December 1, 1946), p. 10.

Unpublished manuscripts, The Estate of the Artist, New York.

RALSTON CRAWFORD: SELECTED GENERAL BIBLIOGRAPHY

Agee, William C. *The 1930s: Painting and Sculpture in America*. Whitney Museum of American Art, New York, October 15–December 1, 1968.

Agee, William C. *Modern Painting in America 1910–1940: Toward a New Perspective*. The Museum of Fine Arts, Houston, 1977.

Boswell, Peyton, Jr. *Modern American Painting*. New York: Dodd, Mead, and Co., 1939.

Davidson, Abraham A. *Early American Modernist Painting*. New York: Harper and Row, 1980.

Friedman, Martin. *The Precisionist View in American Art*. Walker Art Center, Minneapolis, November 13–December 25, 1960.

Friedman, Martin. "The Precisionist View." *Art in America*, vol. 48, no. 3 (Fall 1960), pp. 30–37. Part of a series entitled "The Precisionists," also including: Andrews, Edward Deming, "The Shaker Manner of Building," pp. 38–45; Scully, Vincent J., Jr., "The Precisionist Strain in American Architecture," pp. 45–53; Arnason, H. H., "The New Geometry," pp. 54–61.

Freeman, Richard B. *Niles Spencer*. University of Kentucky Art Museum, Lexington, 1965.

Geldzahler, Henry. *American Painting in the Twentieth Century*. The Metropolitan Museum of Art, New York, 1965.

Janis, Sidney. *Abstract and Surrealist Art in America*. New York: Reynal and Hitchcock, 1944.

Jewell, Edward Alden. "American Painters at the Hotel Marguery Show: A Choice of American Painters." *New York Times*, October 28, 1931, p. 20, Section 7.

Kardon, Janet. *Seventies Painting*. Philadelphia College of Art, April 21–May 21, 1978.

Kootz, Samuel M. *New Frontiers in American Painting*. New York: Hastings House, 1943.

Kramer, Hilton. "The American Precisionists." *Arts,* vol. 35, no. 6 (March 1961), pp. 32–37.

Larkin, Oliver. *Art and Life in America*. New York: Reinhart and Company, 1949.

Maroney, James H., Jr. *Lines of Power*. Hirschl and Adler Galleries, New York, March 12–April 9, 1978.

McCurdy, Charles. *Modern Art: A Pictorial Anthology*. New York: The Macmillan Company, 1958.

McCausland, Elizabeth. "The Daniel Gallery and Modern American Art." *Magazine of Art* (later *The Art Digest*), vol. 44, no. 7 (November 1951), pp. 280–285.

Nordness, Lee, and Weller, Allen. *Art: USA: Now*. C. J. Bucher, Ltd., Lucerne, Switzerland, 1962. Revised edition, New York: Viking Press, 1963.

Pierson, W. H., and Davidson, Martha. *The Arts of the United States*. New York: McGraw-Hill Book Company, 1960.

Ritchie, Andrew C. *Abstract Painting and Sculpture in America*. The Museum of Modern Art, New York, 1951.

Rose, Barbara. *American Art Since 1900*. New York: Fredrick A. Praeger, 1967. Revised edition, 1975.

Stebbins, Theodore E., Jr., and Troyen, Carol. *The Lane Collection, 20th-Century Paintings in the American Tradition*. Museum of Fine Arts, Boston, 1983.

Tsujimoto, Karen. *Images of America, Precisionist Painting and Modern Photography*. San Francisco Museum of Modern Art, September 9–November 7, 1982. Exhibition traveled to The St. Louis Art Museum, December 6, 1982–January 30, 1983; The Baltimore Museum of Art, February 28–March 25, 1983; Des Moines Art Center, May 23–July 17, 1983; Cleveland Museum of Art, August 15–October 9, 1983.

Yeh, Susan Fillin. *The Precisionist Painters 1916–1949: Interpretation of a Mechanical Age*. Heckscher Museum, Huntington, New York, July 7–August 20, 1978.

RALSTON CRAWFORD: ONE-MAN EXHIBITIONS

1934 Maryland Institute of Art, Baltimore.

1937 Boyer Galleries, Philadelphia.

1938 The Philadelphia Art Alliance.

1939 Boyer Galleries, New York.

1942 Flint Institute of Arts, Michigan.

1944 Downtown Gallery, New York.

1946 The Santa Barbara Museum of Art; traveled to M.H. de Young Memorial Museum
of Art, San Francisco; Portland Art Museum, Oregon; Seattle Art Museum, Washington.
Downtown Gallery, New York.

1947 Howard University, Washington, D.C.
Honolulu Academy of Arts.

1949 Cincinnati Art Museum.
University of Minnesota, Minneapolis.
MacMurray College, Jacksonville, Illinois.

1950 Downtown Gallery, New York.
Louisiana State University, Baton Rouge.

1952 Hofstra College, Hempstead, New York.

1953 University of Alabama, Tuscaloosa.
University of Maine, Orono.

1954 Grace Borgenicht Gallery, New York.

1955 E. Weyhe Gallery, New York.
Grace Borgenicht Gallery, New York.
Los Angeles County Museum of Art.

1956 Contemporary Arts Center, Cincinnati Art Museum.
      Grace Borgenicht Gallery, New York.
      Duke University, Durham, North Carolina.

1957 Grand Rapids Art Association, Michigan.
      Davison Art Center, Wesleyan University, Middletown, Connecticut.

1958 Brooks Memorial Art Gallery, Memphis.
      St. George's Gallery Prints, London.
      Milwaukee Art Center.
      Grace Borgenicht Gallery, New York.

1960 A. B. Closson Company, Cincinnati.

1961 University of Kentucky, Lexington.
      San Francisco Museum of Art.
      University of Nebraska, Lincoln.
      Oakland University, Rochester, Michigan.
      Davison Art Center, Wesleyan University, Middletown, Connecticut.
      Lee Nordness Gallery, New York.
      Tweed Gallery, University of Minnesota, Duluth.

1962 University of Maine, Orono.

1963 Nordness Gallery, New York.
      Montgomery Museum of Fine Arts, Alabama.

1965 Sheldon Memorial Art Gallery, University of Nebraska, Lincoln.

1966 University of Illinois, Champaign.

1968 Fine Arts Gallery, Creighton University, Omaha, Nebraska.

1969 Bienville Gallery, New Orleans.
      The Century Association, New York.

1971 Zabriskie Gallery, New York.
      Nordness Gallery, New York.
      Helman Gallery, St. Louis.
      Contemporary Arts Center, Cincinnati Art Museum.

1973 Bienville Gallery, New Orleans.
University of Kentucky, Lexington.
Zabriskie Gallery, New York.
National Collection of Fine Arts, Smithsonian Institution, Washington, D.C.

1974 Sheldon Memorial Art Gallery, University of Nebraska, Lincoln.

1976 Zabriskie Gallery, New York.

1977 Middendorf/Lane Gallery, Washington, D.C.

1978 The Century Association, New York.

1983 University of Maryland, College Park.
The Frederick S. Wight Art Gallery of University of California at Los Angeles.
Hillwood Art Gallery, C. W. Post Center, Long Island University, Greenvale, New York.
The Historic New Orleans Collection, New Orleans.
Robert Miller Gallery, New York.

RALSTON CRAWFORD: COLLECTIONS

Alabama Polytechnic Institute, Auburn.
University of Alabama, Tuscaloosa.
Albright-Knox Art Gallery, Buffalo, New York.
The Baltimore Museum of Art.
The Brooklyn Museum.
Brooks Memorial Art Gallery, Memphis.
The Butler Institute of American Art, Youngstown, Ohio.
Museum of Art, Carnegie Institute, Pittsburgh.
Cincinnati Art Museum.
Art Institute of Chicago.
University of Colorado, Boulder.
Columbus Museum of Art.
University of Delaware, Dover.
The Denver Art Museum.
Des Moines Art Center, Iowa.
The Detroit Institute of Arts.
Duke University, Durham, North Carolina.
Flint Institute of the Arts, Michigan.
Fogg Art Museum, Cambridge, Massachusetts.
Georgia Museum of Art, The University of Georgia, Athens.
Grand Rapids Art Museum, Michigan.
Hamlin College, St. Paul, Minnesota.
Hirshhorn Museum and Sculpture Garden, Smithsonian Institution, Washington, D.C.
Hofstra College, Hempstead, New York.
Honolulu Academy of Art.
Howard College, Washington, D.C.
University of Illinois, Urbana.
Krannert Art Museum, University of Kentucky, Lexington.
University of Illinois, Urbana.
Library of Congress, Washington, D.C.
Los Angeles County Museum of Art.

Louisiana State Art Commission, Baton Rouge.
Louisiana State University, Baton Rouge.
MacMurray College, Jacksonville, Illinois.
University of Maine, Orono.
Manufacturers Hanover Trust Company, New York.
The Metropolitan Museum of Art, New York.
Michigan State University–Oakland, Rochester, Michigan.
University of Michigan, Ann Arbor.
Milwaukee Art Museum.
University of Minnesota, Minneapolis.
University of Minnesota, Tweed Museum of Art, Duluth.
Munson-Williams-Proctor Institute, Utica, New York.
The Museum of Fine Arts, Houston.
The Museum of Modern Art, New York.
National Gallery of Art, Washington, D.C.
National Museum of American Art, Smithsonian Institution, Washington, D.C.
Sheldon Memorial Art Gallery, University of Nebraska, Lincoln.
Neuberger Museum, Purchase, New York.
New York Public Library, New York.
The Newark Museum, New Jersey.
Museum of Art, The University of Oklahoma, Norman.
Philadelphia Museum of Art.
The Phillips Collection, Washington, D.C.
The St. Louis Art Museum.
San Francisco Museum of Modern Art.
Springfield Art Museum, Missouri.
Thyssen-Bornemisza Collection, Lugano, Switzerland.
The Toledo Museum of Art, Ohio.
Vassar College Art Gallery, Poughkeepsie, New York.
Walker Art Center, Minneapolis.
College of Fine Arts, Wesleyan University, Bloomington, Illinois.
Davison Art Center, Wesleyan University, Middletown, Connecticut.
Whitney Museum of American Art, New York.
Wichita Art Museum, Kansas.

Acknowledgments

I especially would like to thank Mrs. Peggy Crawford and Neelon, John, and Robert Crawford for their help in realizing this project. I particularly am grateful to Terry Eagleton of the Crawford Estate for his continuing assistance. In addition, John Cheim, Nathan Kernan, Danielle Tilkin, and Selina Shirley of the Robert Miller Gallery are due my gratitude, as is Linda Lynch. I also wish to thank Virginia Zabriskie for allowing me to consult her files.

WCA
May 1983

DATE DUE